Christ Alive

Christ Alive

*Reflections from the Shadows of
Life into the Light of God*

John Deane-O'Keeffe

RESOURCE *Publications* · Eugene, Oregon

CHRIST ALIVE
Reflections from the Shadows of Life into the Light of God

Copyright © 2025 John Deane-O'Keeffe. All rights reserved. Except for brief quotations in critical publications or reviews, no part of this book may be reproduced in any manner without prior written permission from the publisher. Write: Permissions, Wipf and Stock Publishers, 199 W. 8th Ave., Suite 3, Eugene, OR 97401.

Resource Publications
An Imprint of Wipf and Stock Publishers
199 W. 8th Ave., Suite 3
Eugene, OR 97401

www.wipfandstock.com

PAPERBACK ISBN: 979-8-3852-3660-2
HARDCOVER ISBN: 979-8-3852-3661-9
EBOOK ISBN: 979-8-3852-3662-6
VERSION NUMBER 04/21/25

Scripture quotations are from New Revised Standard Version Bible: Anglicized Edition, copyright © 1989, 1995 National Council of the Churches of Christ in the United States of America. Used by permission. All rights reserved worldwide.

Scripture quotations marked (NIV) are taken from the Holy Bible, New International Version®, NIV®. Copyright ©1973, 1978, 1984, 2011 by Biblica, Inc.™ Used by permission of Zondervan. All rights reserved worldwide. www.zondervan.com. The "NIV" and "New International Version" are trademarks registered in the United States Patent and Trademark Office by Biblica, Inc.

To my wife, Nicola, children, Genevieve, Victoria, Oliver, Georgie, and Cate, and my late parents, Annie and Brendan

The measure of my dreams

And remember that I am with you always, until the end of the age.
Matt 28:20

Contents

Preface | ix

PART 1: REFLECTIONS FROM THE SHADOWS
  Street Life: *My Name Is James: Hear My Name* | 3
  Prisoners? *Hard to Like, Compelled to Love* | 7
  Religion: *Don't Sweat the Small Stuff* | 11
  OMG! You're So Talented: *And . . . ?* | 15
  Call Me Please? *Relax. He Already Did* | 18
  Forgive and Forget: *But How?* | 21
  Status Anxiety: *Seriously . . . What Are We Like?!* | 24
  The Case of Jamie Bulger: *In God's Name . . . Why?* | 27
  Sickness Happens; Healing Follows: *Finding God in a Hopeless Place* | 30
  Unleash Your Inner Saint: *It Could Be You!* | 33
  You, Too, Are a Riot! *So Don't Condemn Others* | 36
  Memories Are Made of This: *Time Fades, God Radiates* | 39
  Perspective Is Everything: *Don't Sweat—God Doesn't* | 42
  For the Love of God: *Give Him a Chance* | 45
  The Nothing People: *Nothing Comes from Nothing—Ask God* | 48
  Annie's Song: *God Is Love and So Are Mothers* | 52
  Putin the Terrible: *Hard to Love, Easy to Hate* | 55
  I Believe! *Or Do I . . .* | 58
  The Evil Within: *Closer Than We Think* | 61
  Every Breath You Take . . . *The God of Communication* | 65
  Sabbath Secrets: *Hiding in Full View* | 69

Contents

When the End Is the Beginning: *Life Ages, Death Restores* | 72
Mind the Dash: *Careful of That Bit Between Birth and Death* | 76
Jaw-Dropping: *Time to Discover the Outer and Inner Cosmos* | 78
Can't Get No Satisfaction? *God Can Help* | 81
You'll Never Walk Alone: *If You Keep Christ in Your Heart* | 84
Judging Others: *For a Living* | 87
Suffer Little Children: *One Boy's Suffering . . .* | 90
Walk On By? *Talking the Talk but Flunking the Walk* | 93
Time to Resolve: *To Do Nothing . . .* | 96
Psycho Killer: *Qu'est-ce que c'est?* | 99
Judge Not . . . *Taking Positions Is for Yoga Instructors* | 102
Making a Criminal? *There but for the Grace of God . . .* | 105
Heroes and Villains? *Boring!* | 108
Call Me by My Name . . . *I Am Worthy* | 111
How Low Can We Go? *Very . . .* | 114
Do You Want to Be in My Gang? *Of Course I Do . . .* | 117
Jimmy Savile: *Hiding in Plain Sight* | 120
Smooth Criminals: *"Meaningless" Is a Movable Feast* | 123

PART 2: THE SEVEN DEADLY SINS
Wrath: *Hold Me Back. Please.* | 129
Pride: *Goes Before You Know What* | 132
Greed: *Who Ate All the Pies? We Did . . .* | 135
Lust? *It's a Tricky One . . .* | 138
Envy: *The Slipperiest of Serpents* | 141
Gluttony: *Have We Bitten Off More Than We Can Chew?* | 144
Sloth? *Cut Your Sloth to Suit Your Measure* | 147
Postscript: Cardinal Virtues: *Don't Perspire the Small Sins* | 150

PART 3: TAKE 5: SERMONETTES FROM THE SHADE
Are You a Thermometer or Thermostat Person?
 Testing the Temperature in Spring | 155
Money Can't Buy You Love | 157
Credible or Incredible? | 159
When We Didn't Have Your Hands, We Had Your Backs | 161
And They Call It Puppy Love . . . | 163

Preface

THIS BOOK OF REFLECTIONS for every week of the year is from the streets, from prisons, from the campus, from church, from people, but most of all, from the heart. It aims to bring the message of faith, hope, and love into the open air of our everyday lives. And just as Jesus walked among us in our daily struggles and joys over two millennia ago, he walks the same paths with us today. These pages reflect the realities of life outside and inside traditional walls, where grace meets grit and where goodness abounds. May these words inspire, uplift, and speak to the journey we all share—in the name of Christ.

John Deane-O'Keeffe
May 2025

Author's Note: The book includes certain material which was first published in both the *Church of Ireland Gazette* and *Church Review*. I am deeply thankful to the editors and readers of both publications for their support and encouragement. Where relevant, these articles have been revised, edited, and expanded for this collection.

Part 1

Reflections from the Shadows

Street Life

My Name Is James: Hear My Name

Recently, I got a notification from my archbishop that he would like me to preach at a service in a place called Christ Church in Dublin—for the commissioning of lay ministers.

Quick as a flash I'm in to the wife to tell her the good news (told by John). "Was he stuck?" she asked. "Stuck?" I said, "Far from it; sure he had a cast of thousands to choose from." "Anyway," I said, "more importantly, how should I pitch it?" "I don't know," came the tired response of someone dealing with this type of validation request on a daily basis. "Why don't you tap into your inner Taylor Swift; that normally works."

Now before anyone gets too concerned, you'll be pleased to hear (or maybe not) that I have decided to leave my inner Swiftie at home for now. However there is one thing that Taylor Swift (apparently) is adept at—and that is that whatever city she plays in, she is rather good at finding out some facts or anecdotes about that place beforehand, and then delivering them to her audience as if she had been living there all her life. So perhaps in this respect (and this respect only, mark you) I might tap into that inner Swiftie after all and refer to a place and people in an inner city area that we will all know, wherever we may be from.

The immediate area where I was preaching in Central Dublin is a tourist nirvana, but it is also a place where some locals struggle hugely with their own lives. There is however, one local in particular I would like to draw your attention to now. James is an addict who lives his life on the streets of North Inner City Dublin, in a line perhaps from what is known as Merchants Quay, right up to a place called Phibsborough Shopping Centre.

I got to know James pretty well over the last few years in my line of work and, additionally, just seeing him tipping around Dublin City Centre.

Part 1: Reflections from the Shadows

One day a while back, I noticed him in the distance up near where he hangs around and I thought to myself, look, I have a fiver in my pocket, he's welcome to that. Last of the big spenders, don't you know. As I was about to pull this fiver out my pocket to give him, I realized (to my absolute horror) that it was actually a fifty euro note that I had folded over. But it was too late—I had committed. More importantly James had seen the color of the note too, and in the manner of a space shuttle having left earth's atmosphere he had truly locked on. Hung for the metaphorical sheep as the lamb, the only thing I asked James at the time to promise me, was that he would not spend *any* of this fifty euro note on food or soft drinks. To which he uttered the immortal words, "John, of that, you can be *absolutely* guaranteed."

I was very much reminded of James from Dublin's North Inner City when considering Ecclesiastes recently when it says, "The Teacher sought to find pleasing words, and he wrote words of truth plainly" (12:10). You see, James was exactly like that—a teacher. Not a "teacher" dressed up like myself in church might be, but James. After all, he *really* spoke kindly to others and no matter what he had, if he could spare it, he would give to others. Maybe even some of my precious fifty euro note come to think of it . . .

On countless occasions I saw him physically helping his fellow addicts on the street when they were in bad shape emotionally or otherwise. Uniquely, he never had a bad word, in my company, to say about anyone else he knew from the street. Instead he spoke only of the kindness of others.

We could all learn a lot from this. Yet why would this simple message be so important for us all as we spend the rest of our lives trying to go to him? Well, because the only word you will ever have to remember as you walk, sometimes trembling through life, is this one word, love. Because, that is James. He is, and always will be, the gold standard for our love—*not* our families, friends, or those we may find easier to love. You see, as God's people, if we truly love James, then we find God. Despise or ignore him, and we must continue our search.

You can only imagine my shock therefore when I tuned into the radio shortly after the demise of my fifty euros to hear the callers talking about a homeless man who had tried to save another from drowning just a short distance from the church where I was preaching in Dublin City Centre. Tragically, in the process, both had lost their lives. That shock soon turned to horror when the name of the man who had died trying to save the other young man was mentioned.

Street Life

Attention: James Nicholl, late of the Irish Defence Forces, of the Curragh, Kildare and latterly, the streets of inner city Dublin.

Callers rang in to say they knew him or had heard of him, and that he was a lovely man. They were right. Some were also angry. Why was this news withheld from the media when we all, however, got to hear in Ireland about the death of our president's second Bernese dog that same weekend but not the tragic passing of these two men? Perhaps, as they say, that is another story.

One thing I can tell you, however. When James Nicholl was alive, no one *ever* paid him the slightest bit of attention. Another so-called junkie, or punk, or street psychopath, around that part of the world, another criminal, another waste of time. But James had a secret hiding in full view, and it was love. Yet most of us, including myself at times, passed him on the streets each day and wouldn't give him a glance, let alone some money.

We shouldn't be surprised by our behaviors. As it says in the Acts of the Apostles, "When [Saul] had come to Jerusalem, he attempted to join the disciples; and they were all afraid of him, for they did not believe that he was a disciple" (Acts 9:26). Hear those words. For they *did not believe* he was a disciple. You are, after all, rarely a prophet in your own land.

Like many followers of the apostles and Christ, James Nicholl had no idea what hate looked like, only giving and caring, yet the rest of us, sadly, often do. And all along, it was he who had everything, and we who had nothing. For he had Christ embedded in his heart. You see, he was not as good as us. In truth, he was the best of us.

The only thing I am going to suggest we have in the forefront of our minds from today onward is to authentically know what Christian love really means (particularly if we don't believe in Christ) as evidenced in James's life, and most especially in his selfless death. You see, although James's life was, in one very real sense, tragic, it was also glorious, for he loved and was loved.

I used to see him sometimes wandering around the Greek Orthodox Church not far from the spot where he died, and after I had heard he had passed, I could not but be reminded of those magnificent final words of the hymn of the Orthodox "Kontakion of the Departed"—words which evidence the sadness of his life and passing, and yet also the joy of his, and for Christians our, resurrection.

> All we go down to the dust; and weeping o'er the grave we make our song:
> Alleluia, alleluia, alleluia.[1]

1. "Kontakion for the Departed," Tone 8, Orthodox Funeral Service (*Euchologion*).

Part 1: Reflections from the Shadows

James's life and countless like his are not lived in vain but rather in the glory of God. It is just we can't see it, for, like Saul, we too were afraid of James, and just didn't believe him. If we only remember one thing in the short time we all spend together on this earth, may it be to believe in the goodness that lies within us all, especially at times and in places where we *least* expect to find it. But one final point if I may: I have one regret regarding James. I never told him that he shared the same first name as one of Jesus' reputed brothers. Now that *would* have been a piece of information that would have pleased him.

Then again—he certainly knows that now.

Prisoners?
Hard to Like, Compelled to Love

You know John's Gospel in part (John 6:56–59) can all sounds a bit "samey," can't it? All that bread of heaven stuff. Sure we have heard all that before, and kind of most Sundays. A diet of bread, week after week, can, after all, get rather tiresome and maybe even a little stale. (Pun intended.) Then it all becomes clearer if we dare to read a little more of this part of John's Gospel. In verse 41, the crowd is whinging. Of course it is. We are always whinging. They complain that he has not come from heaven, because they know his parents. Familiarity is breeding contempt. The crowd's self-assured *knowledge* stands in the way of seeing the truth.

You see, we all suffer from the same difficulty of seeing beyond what we *know* to be true. And apparently we know all about the truth. We know about the poor, about ourselves, about the line separating *the saved* from everyone else, about the sick and the incarcerated. Come to think of it, there is very little we don't seem to know about, because we all have opinions you see. Unfortunately (and as we all also know) opinions are about as useful as a concrete parachute—the more you have, the quicker you're likely to fall to earth. John's Gospel can teach Christians many things, but one is that we need to be a bit more mindful of what we think we have, or know, or accept. And, maybe more importantly, what we think others do not have, or do not know, or do not accept.

Now, of course we would all like to think that we reflect spiritually on how blessed we are in our lives and how others are not. But do we really, and I mean really, accept those who have little? Take a marginalized group that John's Gospel alludes to—prison inmates. They, after all, have nothing. Do we refuse to accept them as the disciples refused to accept Jesus' teachings in John's Gospel?

Part 1: Reflections from the Shadows

Well, let's just have a look at them, shall we? You won't be surprised to hear that, working as a forensic criminologist and as a prison chaplain in a prison in Dublin, I would have a view about all of this. Now, for those of you (perhaps all) who have never stepped inside a prison, descriptions come a poor second, but let's give it a go, shall we? These places are awful, and I mean *really* awful, and here I am talking about them all. Hundreds of (mostly) men are cut off from wider society for an appreciable period of time where they all lead a forced and formally administered round of life. Violence is everywhere, either in the threat or the actuality, and most live in various levels of fear. Drugs are all over prisons (can I repeat that please, all over prisons) and they make everyone's life in there both tolerable and intolerable, in equal measure. In short, feelings of hopelessness and terror, mixed with worthlessness, abound. And this is all on a good day.

Recently, for example, I was met with a mini-riot as I was about to go on one of my landings. The screaming and roaring was followed by a rush of prison officers to break up the fight. Two minutes later, two bloodied men are being led away into segregation protesting their innocence. I talked later with one of the bandaged prisoners, who was now in the punishment block, and I asked what had gone on earlier between him and the other inmate to which he gave the classic response, "We were only messing about. I don't know what the officers were getting so worked up about."

You see, we all see and "accept" things differently. And of course it is not just in my own prison that all of this occurs. On a recent visit to a prison in the UK, within ten feet of where I was standing and in full view of a prison officer, a prisoner stabbed another with a homemade shank—made from a toothbrush. As the victim screamed and fell to the floor, blood pouring from his arm, a prison officer beside us gave out a world-weary sigh of "Here we go again" as he made his way over to join other officers in breaking up the melee. In this prison, as in so many others, violence is a daily occurrence and blood injuries are about as common as the galloping human indifference that prevails.

And of course it's easy, very easy, to blame the prisoners. Yet if we look closely, prisoners seem to have a code. Okay maybe not the Ten Commandments like you are I might claim to have, but a code nonetheless. Now this code, known as the "inmate code," is distinguished more in the breach than the in the observance. I wonder if that sounds familiar, anyone? I mean, it is a noble idea that you would never inform on your fellow prisoners ("snitches get stitches," by the way), and even more commendable that you

Prisoners?

would always pay your debts, share everything, and show loyalty to everyone, but I'll let you in on a little secret: it almost never happens. In fact, if you really wanted to understand what real prison life is like, best put all of that into reverse, and then some.

Which, if you think about it, is very like what happens on the outside with the rest of us. We also have a set of laws or commandments that we claim to honor as best we can, but do we? Okay, maybe we are not out murdering people every day, or maybe not even taking the spouses of others, but that's only two of them.

What about worshiping any "graven image" other than God? Cars, clothes, sports, even our jobs. Have we ever done that? I wonder. What of having no other gods before us? Money, wealth, fame, one-upmanship. We are good on observing that, are we? And then there is the "thou shalt not covet" in the commandments. To covet, remember, means to be so jealous of something someone else has that you want. Coveting makes us miserable and keeps us from putting God first. Sound familiar, anyone?

Actually, the more we go through this list of nonadherence to the commandments the more prisoners don't look any different. Wait a minute. What if they are actually even better than us?! You see, we have a dilemma when it comes to offenders that Gospels like John's stir up. Like the disciples in that Gospel, whether we admit it or not, we too often just can't accept his teachings. Love your neighbor as yourself? How's that going for us? I wonder. Especially when it comes to prison inmates?

Let's get one thing straight however before being accused of wokeism. It is certainly true that some of these inmates do unspeakable things to fellow humans and society in general, so surely we cannot let such deeds go *unpunished*. "Vengeance is mine, I will repay, says the Lord" (Rom 12:19), so by implication, surely then, humans must also take a stand to punish earthly wickedness.

On the other hand, the Bible could not be clearer about how we must consider those in prison "as though in prison with them" for the Lord will want to know if we came to him when he was in prison (Heb 13:3). But there is a question we constantly fail to ask while basking in the glory of failing to accept others in whose shoes we have not walked, and never will.

As Christians we think we broadly accept, for example, prison inmates—but who are we kidding? We are so busy gazing in our mirror we have no time to look out for anyone else, least of all those who have committed crimes. By the way, for the avoidance of any further doubt, nor am

Part 1: Reflections from the Shadows

I a prisoner snowflake. It is fair to say that inmates can often be accused of exactly the same things we fail to do (and then some), and they too will not accept the rules on the outside, or the inside for that matter. I mean, if we were being honest about it all, are prisoners around the world accepting the word of Jesus when he says to us, "It is the spirit that gives life; the flesh is useless. The words that I have spoken to you are spirit and life" (John 6:63)? Well, I'm going to hazard a guess and say no.

But guess what? Neither are we. And remember, most of us have no excuse, but they do. Lots of them. Perhaps in this regard, like the disciples with Jesus in John, before we go back to refusing to ever accept or believe prisoners everywhere, we might leave with one takeaway from life prisoner No. D4510 in my own prison, a prisoner I was talking to only a short time before writing this.

Before I left for the evening recently, I asked him what he was looking forward to most when he is eventually released. His answer? "John, nothing really. Just someone to smile at me."

Religion

Don't Sweat the Small Stuff

"**M**ANY ARE CALLED BUT few are chosen." This is a phrase we are all familiar with and it has just come up again with surprising frequency in religious chatter. But what exactly does it mean? And do we ever give it any time to, how shall we say, let it sink in? Recently, I was invited by a fantastic rector near me to preach at a couple of her harvest services. An even more fantastic 161 souls sat before me at the morning service and almost as many at the evening uniform service, which would, of course, gladden any preacher's heart. I may not have had the nerve to say to them then "that many are called but few are chosen" for fear of alienating the other 160, but for the rest of us maybe more used to lower numbers in our church's each Sunday, that typically won't apply. But as they say on church attendance more generally, that is quite another story.

Specifically, Matthew's Gospel at 22:14 gets me thinking. Well in fairness that is exactly what it is supposed to do. And it got me to thinking about man-made religion and our obsession with it, instead of, for example, that idea of who really gets to enter the kingdom of heaven. Let me try to elaborate. I grew up in a house that was fifty-fifty. No, I don't mean that we were dodgy, though, in fairness, that might have been true too. No, what I mean is that my father's side was Roman Catholic and my mother's, Anglican. Let me explain what this actually looked like.

In the blue corner stood my Roman Catholic father; his brother the Augustinian priest; his sister the Holy Family nun; and his three other spinster sisters, women who were devotees of the sacred heart, St. Christopher, St. Jude, Padre Pio, miraculous medals, and just about any other person or medal you would care to think of. The Shrine at Knock wasn't simply a day out in County Mayo in Ireland, it was lifestyle choice, and woe betide anyone who might question the state of mind of the architect who designed its basilica.

Then in the red corner stood my mother's family. A group I can only described as lapsed Protestant atheists. Nominally Church of Ireland (with a couple of Roman Catholics thrown in there, too, who had "taken the soup"), they were what I would called "recreational reformers." You know the type. They helped out when the other practicing Anglicans were busy: Christmas, Easter, weddings, funerals, that type of thing. My uncle, the Augustinian priest, would say to me that all he could really do for my mother's family was to pray for them. My mother, well, in fairness, I can't repeat her response on these pages. Suffice to say, she didn't agree.

You see, like an episode of that most wonderful of all 1990s British sitcoms, *Father Ted*, my uncle the Augustinian was "mad into the church." Now I'm not talking about any old church here. I am talking about *the* church. In his eyes, the mother church could do no wrong to the point that he (I kid you not) had dinner with General Franco in the Augustinian House in Madrid in the late 1960s shortly before Franco died. When I asked him incredulously a few years later what Franco was like, he uttered the immortal line, "He seemed to be a lovely man, John, and you know he's very good to the church." Hmm. Try telling that to the victims of the "White Terror" in the Spanish Civil War.

However, you see, in my uncle's eyes, being *good to the church* forgave all the horrors that Franco may have committed elsewhere, because being *good* to the church and its clerics is what it was all about. "Many are called, but few are chosen" in his mind meant, okay, maybe the whole world, but in reality, at the end of the day, only the one billion-plus or so Roman Catholics were going to have a look in. As a scriptural foundation, he was especially pleased with the idea of apostolic succession to back up his idea that only a portion of us were likely getting through to the promised land. In other words the Petrine doctrine which says, "You are Peter, and on this rock I will build my church" (Matt 16:18).

Now what does this mean in English? Well it depends on what version of English you are speaking. If it's the Roman Catholic version, then you will believe that bishops have been ordained in a truly unbroken line going back to the apostles. It is this chain of witnesses that perpetuates and preserves the truth of the gospel. The Reformed churches maintain that the Scriptures alone are the infallible rule of faith and that all believers are competent to interpret them. The word is sufficient (albeit it may not be

Religion

alone) for many. This is why you can have upward of twenty thousand Protestant denominations in the US alone. Anyone can set up a church in God's eyes. The main thing that's important is the individual, not the church. So we Anglican types are having our theological cake and choking on it. We have a position that is a blend of the two sides of this interpretation. We accept that both are true. It was about Peter and it was about his succession. Succession is good for the church's *well-being* we say but *not* its *being*. Truthfully, the amount of splinters we have in the you know where from sitting on that fence is frightening.

My lovely Augustinian uncle, however, had the Catholic doctrinal thing right to a T. Church first (because of apostolic succession), individuals second. So there is only one Roman Catholic denomination, and that would be, well . . . Roman Catholic. So certain theologians get very exercised about Matthew's Gospel because they really, and I mean really, think it's very, very important. And I repeat that critical line: "Many are called, but few are chosen." All of which must come as a great shock to the Muslims, Sikhs, Hindus, and even Buddhists, God help us, who must feel very left out.

Hang on a moment though. Could it really be that God actually chose all of us Christians to be part of the small group of the saved ones by sheer luck of our birthplace and family situations? Well, if you don't mind, in response to that I would now like to use a nontheological phrase that you won't hear too often in schools of religion or from divinity faculties around the world. We need to get a grip. If we honestly think that the loving Christian God that we purport to know and follow is busy selecting human beings like lotto tickets on the basis of whether we believe, half-believe, or don't believe at all in apostolic succession—or the ability or otherwise of Our Lady of Fatima to find our driver's license—well, we probably need to go back to Sunday school. Yes, we all have our religion. Let's now enjoy it, practice it, and revere it as our pathway. After all, our Christian faith is undoubtedly what was given to us, so it is our obligation to practice it just as it may be the obligation of a young man from Yemen to follow Islam and a woman from Sri Lanka to be Buddhist. I'll even let you in on a little secret. All the theology that I have studied still only ever comes back to one word, love, and here's what we mean by that. The most important person we will ever meet in our Christian lives will never be a theologian wrestling with apostolic succession or who may or may not be chosen (and you'll have to trust me on that one). Instead, *the* most important person is the man or woman who lives in their boots while they ask for change outside an off-license to get some drink and/or drugs to numb their pain. Indeed, the only line we may need to actually remember is from Isaiah, one we mostly overlook so busy are we with the perennial favorite catch phrase from Matthew: "Then the Lord God will wipe away the tears from all faces, and the disgrace of his people he will take away from all the earth, for the Lord has spoken" (Isa 25:8).

So the next time we are going to get some groceries and are pretending not to see a fellow human being on their knees in front of us, I suggest that it may be *this* message of God's love and compassion in Isaiah which will be a more useful one for us all to remember. Perhaps more useful than wondering which ones of us around the world will be actually saved or not according to our chosen or given faith. Frankly, in one very real sense, none of that is any of our business. The reality remains that we are all called by God. It is now up to us to decide in our daily lives if we will be the ones deserving of his choosing.

OMG! You're So Talented
And . . . ?

I KNOW, I KNOW WHAT you're all thinking. For the love of God, John, you are saying, What *is* the parable of the talents about in Matthew? Okay, maybe you weren't thinking that right now, but you need to. We've heard it before alright, but we only have a vague enough notion what it might be getting at. Something to do with some guys having more talents than other guys, and at the end someone is getting thrown into the pit of despair where his (or her) false teeth are gnashing while other parts are wailing. All in all, a bit confusing with hardly what could be described as a great ending.

But let's start with the word *talent*, shall we. Now there's a word that's become somewhat diluted—part of the dilution of our English language that we are getting used to. Take the word *legend* for example. Time was if you were described as a legend you were busy slaying dragons and demons in the underworld with your sword, or at the very least pulling it out of a very large rock indeed. Cut to the current day, and now, you're a legend if you manage to bring back the correct flavor of snack from your local supermarket. That poor word *talent*, too, has taken an equal battering. Once, if you were talented it meant you had a very specific skill in a certain area or areas such as medicine, law, acting, or you were a skilled artisan of some sort. Today, you have talent if you can post a picture of yourself up on Instagram with your tongue sticking out and call yourself a "serious influencer."

It seems that today everyone is talented, and some of us don't like that idea. I mean, if everyone is talented, no one is talented, we cry. Did you come last in the egg and spoon race at school? You really won. Failed your exam? Don't worry, it was just the questions didn't suit you. Didn't get that job interview? I heard they were a horrible company to work for anyway, so you had a lucky escape. The idea of *talent* has become a movable feast and it's hard to think of anyone who may not be talented by our measurements today. But just hold that thought for a moment. In biblical times, and in the context of Matthew's parable, a talent was a large unit of money. Perhaps worth some twenty-five thousand euros or dollars each in today's money. Not to be sniffed at.

The premise of the parable of the talents is simple enough too. A rich man delegates the management of his wealth to his servants, much as investors in today's financial markets do. He gives five talents (for argument's sake—one hundred thousand euros or dollars) to the first servant, two talents to the second, and one talent to the third. Two of the servants earn 100 percent returns by trading with the funds, but the third servant hides the money in the ground and earns nothing. The rich man returns, rewards the two who made money, but severely punishes the servant who did nothing.

So what's God saying? Surely Christ isn't saying that if you are weak at investing money in this life then you are doomed in the next? No, not quite, but what he is saying is that he has given us a wide variety of gifts and we are expected to use them, to the full, and in his name. Not squander them or leave them to waste. And you know, sometimes, despite what we might think, it's not obvious who's wasting their God-given gifts and who's using them to the full. For example, I met an Irish Traveller named Brigid recently in a major teaching hospital where I am working with the chaplaincy team. She was using all the talents God gave her to the maximum, and, yes, in his name. And yet I can guarantee you that everyone she meets thinks the exact opposite. Brigid was out drinking with her friends on a recent Saturday night—a girls' night out. She's forty-seven years old and would pass for a woman twenty years her senior. She inexplicably developed a pain in her side and she ended up in ED a few days later, and when I met her, was in early liver and kidney failure.

Her life has been a car crash. A father who abused her, and then a husband who did the same, and then left her and the family. She has had three sons, one of whom died in her arms three years ago from an accidental drug overdose. He was twenty-one. Her two other sons, who are also in their twenties, are in prison serving sentences for drug dealing and armed robbery. She is now going into liver and kidney failure. But you know what? I think she must have read Matthew's Gospel a while back, for she has love and Christ in her heart and used this key talent to its full. All she talked to me about was her belief, her faith journey, the love of God which has no limits, and how blessed she had been in her life to have such love from her family and friends. I repeat, how blessed *she* had been, even after the life she has had and is still having. You see Brigid *is* the parable of the talents.

So don't go away from this thinking Christ wants us just to study hard in school and college, work hard to get and keep our jobs, rise up our professions, and then in retirement do a few good deeds before we fall off our perch, and all will be well. That's nice, but it's not the full picture. Indeed it may not be any of it. God has given each of us a wide variety of gifts and he expects us to employ those gifts in his service, not our own. It is not acceptable merely to put those gifts we may have on a closet shelf and ignore them or use them to further our own little lives. Whatever we do, we must do it for him. If we get nothing else out of Matthew's parable of the talents, we should think of Brigid, the seriously ill Irish Traveller woman in that hospital, who is doing exactly what God asks of her and her talents.

The only question that remains for us is, are we?

Call Me Please?
Relax. He Already Did

As a student, I had the unrivaled pleasure of working at the butcher's counter in our local supermarket. My boss was a purveyor of daily optimism alongside which he would position some "great one-liners" as only he would call them. One of his favorites was when an elderly woman might come to the counter and inquire if the fish were fresh. "Madam," he would brace himself, "many are cold, but few are frozen." See what I mean? Okay, you probably had to be there.

I thought about him recently and the idea of who might he chosen by God (leaving aside fish for now) when not one but two religious programs appeared on a local television network. Religious programs on mainstream TV have become such a rare event they deserve a mention. The first was ominously titled "The Last Priests in Ireland" only to be swiftly followed by, wait for it, "The Last Nuns in Ireland." If you didn't know better, you might think that the Irish national broadcaster were telling us something.

They are worth a viewing though. It is not that they are necessarily the most brilliantly produced or put together pieces of work that have ever been assembled, which, as we all know, might be a rare enough event when it comes to religious programming anywhere. The male narrator, too, certainly had his charms, but (perhaps because he is an actor) he looked at times like he was a security guard in a warehouse who's just got a fright, such was his shock at the decline of Catholicism in Ireland. The female journalist did her best on the nuns' side, but on a number of occasions during the documentary she looked as if she might actually pass out on her own sincerity. Listening to a poet who was also wheeled out, one felt at times that we might be walking through mercury as he delivered some homespun philosophical and theological truths to us while wearing a cheesecloth shirt and looking more like a confused teenager than a wise bard.

Yet for all of this the programs did have some interesting little gems in there for us. One very certain priest, when asked how he felt about the decline of Roman Catholic vocations to the priesthood in Ireland from some fourteen thousand to four thousand over a few decades, replied that he was "delighted." Delighted because, to paraphrase, "there was too many of us, and we were part of an exclusive club of male celibates, a club that no one else could join. This new club will be for everyone, equally."

There was also some skirting around the issue of the superiority that existed among Roman Catholic priests by virtue of the simplistic allure of the Latin expression *noli me tangere* translated as "do not touch." This statement has arguably kept priests as separate, distinct, and frankly better than their flock over the centuries. And there was one other very important topic that kept arising in the documentaries and is evidenced in, for example, Mark's Gospel. That of the special calling that these priests and nuns felt was theirs. A "special" calling no less.

Now before any member of *any* Christian denomination watches these documentaries and says, well that is the Roman Catholic, that is not us, I would ask us all to take the five-hundred-year-old oak tree out of all our eyes before any of us start criticizing any other set of beliefs—Catholic or otherwise.

Many of the issues that came up are of importance to all Christians, commissioned ministers, congregations, and paid or, indeed, non-paid up members of any church. And one matter is especially glaring—namely that of a so-described "calling." It's not just Roman Catholic priests or nuns that talk about having a calling, believe you me. Other Christian clergy and ministers talk about it constantly. Some had epiphanies that drew them to God, some others apparently had a slow, gradual move toward God, while I'm guessing a few others weren't exactly sure where else they could get a job.

But just like in the Roman Catholic tradition, members of other Christian churches too like to talk about their special calling. Now that is not to deny that such men and women have been called. God help us, perhaps it even applies to myself. That we are called to preach and teach and hopefully, here and there, bring some hope and maybe occasionally joy into people's lives is something of a given. So let all clergy and lay ministers around the world give themselves a pat on the back for what they are doing, or, perhaps in some cases at least, believe they're doing.

Part 1: Reflections from the Shadows

But none of this is really the point. The fact that people like me, and people far more elevated, may have a fashion of a faith calling does not mean that everyone else doesn't have the same—or indeed a much higher calling to God. After all, what makes a Christian minister's or pastor's call to God's service any more or less special or different than that of a plasterer, a bus driver, a homemaker, or a deep-sea diver? Remember you heard this here today. Absolutely nothing.

The truth is that many clergymen and women of every denomination could learn a lot from the "ordinary folk" they may sometimes unwittingly feel they have the edge over. Denial, as they say in certain parts of Dublin, is not just a river in Egypt. "Follow me," Jesus said to his disciples in Mark's Gospel, "and I will make you fishers of men" (Matt 4:19). Now for the avoidance of any doubt, the definition of a disciple is one who is a personal follower of Christ, which most certainly includes every single one of us. Not just the people you may see up on the plinth on any given Sunday. The problem with those within perhaps all Christian traditions, is that many really did think they were better than everyone else and that God had somehow especially chosen them. A type of "favorite child syndrome" occasionally mixed up with a "savior complex." Sorry to burst any such person's bubble but God loves us all dearly and, most importantly, equally. If you have a calling to lead in a church then off you go, but please try not to *lord* it over others on Sundays (see what I did there?).

So if you're called to be a plumber, will you please make sure you tighten the pipes properly before you leave? A lawyer, don't forget to put that money in the client account and not your own. A doctor, at least try and look as if you know what you're talking about and are vaguely interested in us. Long-term unemployed? Keep fighting, for God is at your side. We all have different skills, and with them we all have different callings, and no one calling is superior to the next for they are all equal in God's eyes once we follow his path.

So from today let us all leave our nets, whatever they may be, and follow Jesus as his disciples did and stop fretting about whose calling may be better or more important than the next one. None of them are. The only call that matters is our personal calling to live the Christian life, and here and there, in whatever position we occupy (or, indeed, do not occupy) let's see if we can gently convince others of the same message of love. Thinking you are better than someone else because you are a clergyperson or religiously inclined is not what God's calling is about. Authentically humbling yourself before all others, however, most certainly is.

Forgive and Forget
But How?

Forgiveness is a great word today. At least for half of civilization. The other half, mind you, is busy saying that you must not forgive and you must never forget all or any wrongs that were and are done to you, and the very best way to do this is to seek revenge. Revenge may be a dish best served cold, but whether cold, warm, or piping hot, this group would have us believe that it must nonetheless be served. Ask the battered people of Ukraine or the Middle East or Somalia, or the families of those children that were sent to eternity by a so-called school shooter, or, indeed, those in Ireland who suffered so grievously during the so-called Troubles. Ask any of them to just "let go" and I'm sure many might not be long telling you what exactly you can do with your forgiveness. You see, forgiving is all very well if its someone's problem over there. But what if you are the parent who says goodbye to their son at 8:00 p.m. as he goes out with some friends for the evening only six hours later to be holding his still warm body in a morgue after some wanton, random attack? Forgiveness here is not only difficult; it is impossible. Then the other half of us seem to talk about little else then forgiving everyone, and everything, always, and in all circumstances, regardless of how difficult it may be. In the manner of the musical *Frozen*, they are the experts in letting things go, while the rest of us are performing choke holds on the last person we imagine looked at us sideways.

It's all a bit of a mess really. One group is waiting (dare I say, hoping) to be insulted and offended so they can unleash their unmerciful wrath on that person or persons, while the other lot are wandering around Gandhi-like in their flip flops hoping that we can all just give peace a chance, sure it's nothing that a nice cup of tea wouldn't fix in any event.

Part 1: Reflections from the Shadows

So the art of forgiveness presents us broken humans with something of a dilemma to say the least. Throw Christ into the mix and we add yet another variable into this melting pot. Or do we? I mean, for example, Matthew's Gospel message at 18:21–22 is pretty straightforward if you think about it. Peter came and said to Christ, "'Lord, if another member of the church sins against me, how often should I forgive? As many as seven times?' Jesus said to him, 'Not seven times, but, I tell you, seventy times seven.'" Think for one moment, if you will, of the person you currently most dislike for whatever reason, living or dead. Have you got that? You know who it is.

Well not only must you forgive them wholly and entirely for whatever wrong you perceive they have done to you, you must forgive them seventy times seven. You see in this parable of the unforgiving servant, Peter thinks forgiving seven times will impress Jesus. He wasn't even 10 percent there. I hear what you are thinking. That's not forgiveness—that's divinity. And, after all, we are only human. Yet whatever way we shake it up, forgiveness remains at the heart of what it means to follow Christ. At the core of our inability to authentically forgive lies one emotion and that is anger. And anger is like an animal crouching at our doors morning, noon, and night. As that wonderful pastor Tim Mackie advises in his lectures, Christ-like forgiveness on the other hand is a new and different humanity, one that is unbridled with mercy, not anger.[1]

Now I think I know what some of you may be thinking: John, you're a funny man for the big statements, and it's all very well and good, but I'm a very busy person and I don't know if I have the time, energy, or inclination left at the end of any given day for all that forgiving malarkey. Anyway, you might say, I'd be making a fool of myself if I were to forgive everyone, for everything. Well, I think we may all need to reflect on what that moment of forgiveness really meant in the Gospel of Matthew. As Tim Mackie once more advises, there is no biblical evidence that we are aware of where Jesus says that forgiveness means ignoring or forgetting a perceived wrong done to you.[2] Sometimes called the "doormat" misunderstanding, forgiving "seventy-seven" times (or any variant) does not mean suffering in silence. No. You talk to that person, and you talk to others. Neither in his life, nor at that beautiful moment of forgiveness in that Gospel, does Jesus say we

---

1. Tim Mackie, "Forgiveness," *The Bible Project*, Matthew series, episode 27, Tim Mackie Archives, Aug. 19, 2017, YouTube video, https://www.youtube.com/watch?v=c8907NaR7zI&t=1000s.

2. Mackie, "Forgiveness," https://www.youtube.com/watch?v=c8907NaR7zI&t=1224s.

must condone or excuse clear wrongs. He never asks us to say it's not a big deal or it doesn't matter. Nor does he say that we should tolerate or allow further abuse, perhaps the most common misunderstanding. Jesus does not envisage that you will be alone with that person again, especially if it is a dangerous situation.

In other words, forgiving all those times does not mean you get back in the arena of battle.

Nor, if I can be so bold, should we overly obsess about reconciliation or restoration. What is it going to take for you and that person you fell out with to reconcile? I'm guessing a lot of work, and that's okay. Jesus asks us to forgive, but what we cannot do is control an apology or reconciliation. Sometimes it is impossible as the person may have died or the relationship is too dangerous. You see, in the final analysis, forgiveness does not take two. It's we who do it in our hearts. Jesus came among us and personally absorbed the sin we have created in his good world when he died for us on the cross. When we forget this, we think we occupy a higher moral ground than someone else.

Tim Mackie, once again, has it spot on. When we don't forgive, what we have actually done is take that person's complex humanity and boil it down to the *one* thing that they did to me. They lied to me once, so now they *are* a liar. They cheated me, so now they *are* a cheater. This is what we do. We demonize others. Regardless, forgiveness is a choice, and when we forgive we give up "a right" to retaliate, for we remember God's forgiveness for us.[3]

Perhaps this is all best encapsulated in one moment of both horror and love. Some of you may remember the horror of a mass shooting in Charleston, South Carolina, and nine worshiping Americans were killed during Bible study at Mother Emanuel African Methodist Episcopal Church. The daughter of one of the victims, Nadine Collier, came to the media and spoke directly to the person who had committed this atrocity and said: "I forgive you. I want everyone to know that. You took something very precious from me. You hurt me. You hurt a lot of people. But if God forgives you, I forgive you."[4]

Now that, dear reader, is forgiveness. No more excuses.

---

3. Mackie, "Forgiveness," https://www.youtube.com/watch?v=c8907NaR7zI&t=2580s.

4. Associated Press Charleston, "Representatives of Charleston Shooting Victims 'Forgive' Dylann Roof," *Guardian*, June 20, 2015.

Status Anxiety
Seriously . . . What Are We Like?!

YOU KNOW, AS I read through parts of Matthew's Gospel, I note a recurring theme. That of never getting ahead of ourselves and always keeping grounded in what really matters in life. In truth, I can never help but feel that all of us may have fallen at the first fence before we have even begun. You might say that it was ever so. After all, in chapter 15 of Matthew's Gospel the disciples shunned the Canaanite woman because of her annoying cries; they disdained her mannerisms, her status as a gentile, and her demon-possessed daughter. Oh, and of course there was that small matter that she was a woman, an offense in itself. You see, women had little standing in a society that needed men to serve as intermediaries in legal and spiritual matters. And it gets worse. Since she was a gentile, the Jews saw her as not only unsaved but also unworthy of salvation, while of course viewing themselves as terrifically worthy. However, at times, we can all generally decide that Christ didn't, of course, really mean us to take all of this literally in Matthew. More a metaphorical message, we say to ourselves. Some vague notion that we mustn't get ahead of ourselves in life, that we are not better than anyone else. This is much more palatable.

The truth is, of course, that despite the clear teaching of the gospel, we human beings remain obsessed and occupied with what we imagine to be our own elevated status above others. Speaking to status anxiety, during the course of any given year I lecture in a prestigious UK university, and during those times I get to meet all sorts. I say all sorts. What I really meet is all sorts—of one type, of course. Don't get me wrong, they're all a very lovely group of US, UK, and other students of all age ranges. While they are there to learn and get credits, they are also there to experience the place with its dreamy spires and effortlessly shabby professors with their even shabbier dress sense. (Yours truly excluded, of course.) When they come there, they especially look forward to dinner each evening in what is a magnificent dining area. Think Harry Potter meets Enid Blyton.

Now, most of these students are open-jawed for most of their meal and marvel at how well they are doing in life. And they are. However, the real measure of your success in all such places is not that you simply attend the evening meal in wonderful surroundings where you can doubtless feel rather good about yourself. The real goal (like occurs in Matthew's Gospel with the disciples) is to prove publicly that you may be better than everyone else. In this instance, this can mean sitting at what is known as "High Table." Now High Table does exactly what it says on the tin. It's a table that is, well, high, but most importantly higher than the rest. At it tend to sit great luminaries (present company included), and each evening certain students are invited to join such colossally important individuals. On certain evenings you can have a final High Table where I can safely say that everyone generally looks so delighted with their lives that, as they say in Ireland, if they were bars of chocolate, they would have eaten themselves.

Many years ago, at such an evening, one of my mature students came to me and whispered in my ear that there appeared to be a catastrophic mistake. She was not listed as a guest at High Table that evening. Further investigation into this terribly serious matter revealed that as she already sat at High Table earlier in the week, that was all she was getting. I am not exaggerating when I say her face collapsed to the floor, her shoulders become hunched and she walked back to the "ordinary" tables, looking like a woman who had been told she had won the lottery only to be advised five minutes later that it was in fact a five-dollar cash card. For the record, the lady in question was a retired business consultant, and a lovely person as well. You see, sometimes, just sometimes, we can all get ahead of ourselves and forget what is real.

The reality is, however, that whatever way we might like to distance ourselves from behaviors such as these, and such as evidenced in Matthew's Gospel toward the Canaanite woman and her ill daughter, we are all at it. Day in and day out. We are obsessed with how we may rank in our professional lives regarding our qualifications; our pre-nominals and our post-nominals; the money we earn; the place we live; the friends we have; the clothes we wear; the restaurants we visit; the jewelry and items we hoard; and yes, even, and maybe especially, the churches we all attend. Yet the message of the Canaanite woman in Matthew's Gospel is not, however, just a take-it-or-leave-it wellness mantra about humility. It has a far more important, and significant, message for Christians. None of our status anxiety, or how we perceive ourselves in any human pecking order, matters. I repeat, *none* of it.

We can harvest, launder, or iron all the money we want but when the bell tolls for us, it will not chime to the rustle of our banknotes, or, indeed, to the perceived majesty of our human position but only to one thing— whether we loved, and, if lucky, were loved. We can secure that job title or promotion, cement our position in the residents committee, or even, dare I say it, reach dizzy heights in our church, and still *the* most important person we will ever meet sits on the cold ground while asking for change to get some vodka and/or drugs to numb *their* pain. The only question to ask ourselves in this life is therefore, How will we *really* meet others who are on the floor like the Canaanite woman from the comfort of *our* world view? As Matt 15:21–28 implicitly asks of us, When *we* give our own banquets (real or metaphorical) will we invite the poor? The crippled? The lame and the blind of this world? Or will we instead spend our remaining years worrying about whether we get to yet another meaningless High Table in this broken world we, not Christ, have created?

Let me leave you with one final thought from psychiatrist Carl Jung who had a seminal piece of advice for all of us obsessed with looking upward in life to find meaning. The reason he said that modern man fails to find God is that we consistently fail to look low enough.[1] The time has surely passed for us all to come down off our High Tables and instead get on our knees.

---

1. For more about the importance of engaging with the unconscious and shadow aspects of the psyche, see Carl Jung, *Alchemical Studies*, vol. 13 of *The Collected Works of C. G. Jung*, ed. and trans. Gerhard Adler and R. F. C. Hull (Princeton, NJ: Princeton University Press, 1982). Of particular relevance is "The Philosophical Tree."

The Case of Jamie Bulger
In God's Name . . . Why?

READERS OVER FORTY-FIVE YEARS of age will have the image of the innocent face of two-year-old Jamie Bulger forever etched in their memory. Younger readers, too, will doubtless have heard of this appalling murder. This taking of life was beyond compare and left us all with a sense of hopelessness for the human condition like few others. Jamie Bulger was from Kirkby in Merseyside, Liverpool, in the UK, and was abducted from the New Strand Shopping Centre in Bootle on February 12, 1993.[1] His mother was briefly distracted and during this time he was taken by two ten-year-old schoolboy friends, Robert Thompson and Jon Venables. The journey of terror they took Jamie Bulger on was of some 2.5 miles, and during this time he was both physically (and almost certainly) sexually assaulted by one or more of the boys. They were seen in this journey by some thirty-eight adult witnesses yet only two challenged the older boys and they were easily fobbed off by Thompson and Venables who presented as older than their years.

Two-year-old James Bulger was punched and kicked by both boys and almost certainly it was Robert Thompson who literally dropped the small child on his head on the canal bank. At the railway track, where he was eventually to die, he was kicked, stamped, and beaten by both boys who threw stones at him and poured blue paint over his face. Finally a twenty-two pound iron bar was dropped on him. Thompson and Venables then laid his body over the railway track to make it look like an accident had occurred. The facts are almost too unbearable to recount and those of us who watched matters unfold on TV and the radio at time could simply

---

1. Wikipedia, "Murder of James Bulger," last modified Jan. 13, 2025, https://en.wikipedia.org/w/index.php?title=Murder_of_James_Bulger&oldid=1269150406.

not believe what had occurred. Jamie Bulger had just endured his road to Calvary. He was two years of age.

Later in the year, Thompson and Venables became the youngest children in British legal history to be found guilty of murder. The Parole Board at the time made them subject to a lifelong license. They were however released at eighteen years of age with full anonymity following a European Court of Human Rights ruling. Britain and Ireland were in uproar. What had made such seemingly innocent boys commit so heinous an act? The explanation on the lips of many were that the two friends were "evil" and so no public sympathy or judicial latitude should be afforded them. The narrative was that they knew what they were doing and still went ahead and did it, and so should be punished temporally (and one assumes eternally). So two bad, mad, and probably sad boys had gotten their comeuppance. Case closed. It was a tidy wrap up for those unaccustomed to the notion that God's world is never black or white but a mixture of more grays than we can ever imagine.

It was true that both boys had shown signs of premeditation. They had spoken to each other about getting a child "lost" and two weeks before the abduction Jon Venables was seen to be observing children in the shopping center; on the day of the abduction, too, both boys were seen to be watching children, as if selecting a target. There was evidence, too, that Jon Venables (at least) had seen a popular horror cult movie at the time, *Child's Play 3*, which featured a psychopathic doll, Chucky, and so may have replicated those behaviors in the killing of Jamie. The media were thus very busy at the time playing out a roller-coaster narrative on the debilitating effect that violent computer games were having on young children. Pointing the finger at uncomplicated and tidy explanations for such a horror soon became the low-hanging fruit of public discourse.

Less time however was spent in newspaper print or radio talk time examining the backgrounds of both Robert Thompson and Jon Venables. If they had, they may have found some better clues. While it is true to say that chaos can sadly surround many children's lives and yet they do not progress to commit crime of the type committed by Thompson and Venables, that is perhaps to miss the point. For both these boys their backgrounds were marked at the extreme end of mayhem. For Jon Venables, instability marked his childhood where both mother and father suffered from clinical depression. Any attention that was given was only offered to his younger siblings, and incontrollable rages marked his school experience according to teachers.

Robert Thompson, too, had a childhood defined by extreme turbulence. His family was classically dysfunctional. His mother was beaten by her father when she was a child, and she then went on to marry Robert (senior) who then violently abused her. He permanently left the family home and so young Robert had now witnessed endemic domestic violence and he, too, had been abandoned. Like Jon Venables, any investment there is in the house is toward his younger siblings while he receives zero love and affection. Unlike his friend, however, Thompson is described as a "cool" customer and not easily ruffled. The meeting of these two catastrophically dysfunctional child personalities arguably created the prefect criminogenic storm. A storm that was to leave a two-year-old boy brutally murdered and a public baying for more childhood blood.

The trope of "throwing away the key" may have its superficial charms, but not only does it sit uneasily with Christ's message, it eviscerates it. That both Robert Thompson and Jon Venables committed one of the most horrendous murders on these islands in living memory is indisputable. That they could carry out such an act while they were both only ten years of age is unfathomable. Indeed, that we as a public at the time were searching for justice in the haze of this unspeakable horror, is also clear.

Yet we do not diminish Jamie Bugler's life and death by showing compassion toward Robert Thompson and Jon Venables. On the contrary, we do far more by being compassionate at the very time they least appear to deserve it. We, too, must be gracious and compassionate, slow to anger and full of love and faithfulness (Ps 51:1). These boys were hard to love then, and, indeed, this difficulty for us continues as Jon Venables has since been convicted of further unspeakable crimes. But love them we must, and that is not a challenge to us as Christians. It is a command. If we cannot do it for ourselves, we must at least do it for the short life of Jamie Bulger.

He, and the God with whom he now rests, deserve no less from us.

Sickness Happens; Healing Follows

Finding God in a Hopeless Place

Now back in the early 1980s, eighteen-year-old boys didn't like to admit having any pain. Perhaps I should clarify. Every eighteen-year-old boy except me, that is. Pain and I were never the best of friends and the smallest twinge, or even a cousin of a twinge, could send yours truly to the ED. Leaving aside the pain, there was of course the small matter that a "small" twinge could be a portent of the Four Horsemen (and groupies) of the Apocalypse. Don't sweat the small stuff, the pop psychologists advised us. I don't think so, sister. Now that's the stuff you *really* need to sweat.

But back to eighteen-year-old John. When I got a small pain in my right side in 1982, I therefore assumed Beriberi, the bubonic plague, or malaria. Or possibly, all three. Considering my self-diagnosed catastrophic physical condition, I managed to travel at some speed to our family doctor based in Dublin, a gentle man from Belfast—a cross between Mother Teresa and Tammy Wynette.

"I think you have a wee touch of appendicitis there, John," he said. "A wee touch?" says I, "So not too bad then, Doctor?" "Well, you will live all right, but we had better get it removed," he said with the casual abandon of someone who clearly wasn't about to have their own appendix removed. Seemingly, I fainted with the news (I kid you not) so that the poor GP had to drive a semiconscious, dribbling teen in his cheesecloth shirt and flares up to the now forgotten Adelaide Hospital, Dublin, for admission.

Here I remember seeing a lot of nurses in giant wimples, all who looked every bit as worried as I was, thus of course confirming that they knew something I long suspected. I could not be long for this world. By

Sickness Happens; Healing Follows

some quirk of fate I recovered (within two days) and was back home advising anyone who would listen that it was by the grace of God they all still had me. "The Lord moves in mysterious ways," I wisely told my parents as they raised their eyes to heaven in sheer pity for this curious boy sitting before them.

Cut to many years later and this peculiar young boy is certainly still peculiar, but definitely more ancient and now, along with others, trying to sometimes care to the pastoral needs of patients in hospital and prison. And what an experience. For you think you have seen all the suffering possible, until you haven't. You think no day can get worse, and then it does. You also think you may never meet Christ in such a terrible milieu as a hospital, but you do, and everywhere. And you believe you will never know joy in such a place, and yet you were so very wrong.

Take Tom whom I met in my chaplaincy journey recently for example. During one evening duty, I went to ICU and in the waiting area outside I noticed a middle-aged woman and man sitting and I made myself known to them. They advised that their husband and brother, Tom, was just back in ICU having undergone a very serious heart operation and further related procedures. They revealed that he was a man who read the Bible daily and had a particular affinity for the Psalms. Especially, his wife advised, Ps 52.

On arriving in the room I noticed that the patient was intubated and had many other medical accruements as would be expected from someone who had just returned from major open-heart surgery. His nurse was with him and was busy attended to him as I went in. She advised that Tom had just come back from major surgery and so he would be unable to respond or engage in *any* manner. However, I was, she advised, free to pray at his bedside. Tom appeared unconscious as he was heavily sedated. As I introduced myself to him, I noticed that he had "Psalm 52" emblazoned across his chest. As I then began to read Ps 52, Tom's right leg began to twitch. About midway through the Psalm, he slowly raised his left arm to head height and partially opened his eyes. He also appeared to be mouthing the words "thank you," or some other form of acknowledgment.

As I walked along the empty and perfectly still corridor between ICU and HDU afterward, I looked again at Ps 52 and one line struck me: "And I will hope in your name, for your name is good" (Ps 52:9 NIV). And suddenly both myself and the world around me seemed very small yet I felt like one of its most blessed people.

Part 1: Reflections from the Shadows

I met with Tom subsequently, when he was doing much better and about to be discharged, and I learned much about him and what he hopes his future years will bring. He is a scriptural Leviathan, yet this is a weight he carries lightly. He remained unsurprised and entirely composed by his chronic illness and the episode when the Holy Spirit moved among both of us that evening, for, as Hebrews tells us, his faith remains the confidence of what he hopes for, and the assurance for that which he does not see (Heb 11:1). Tom is a warrior and, as Peter tells us, a warrior who is after God's heart is a man of authenticity (1 Pet 2:8). I could have done with Tom in the GP's surgery all those years ago . . .

The suffering of patients like Tom in hospital, and, indeed, in prisons, and their resolute faith, show us the way, the truth, and the life in all its human Technicolor, and in so doing can draw us closer into the arms of God. A God who, incidentally, can curiously appear at times to be unavailable in all the human suffering we see. Yet all we really have to do is listen to John.

> Little children, let us love, not in word or speech, but in truth and action (1 John 3:18).

You see, this patient Tom, like Christ, has a secret hiding in full view. Like all God's children, he reflects the Christ incarnate with all the failings, problems, and suffering that being human entails. Yet in the darkest corners of suffering he, and patients like him, should remain the measure of all our dreams.

And to think, all that he, and I, ever needed was the love of Christ. Long may it continue.

Unleash Your Inner Saint
It Could Be You!

Now, I'm hoping it won't have escaped your attention that each year lots of people celebrate St. Patrick's Day. You may have heard about it in the news . . . especially in Ireland, and the US, of course. It's a grand feast day and one we celebrate every year. It feels kind of important and, well, it is. But some fun facts about St. Patrick before we begin.

He wasn't, of course, even Irish (probably Welsh), and he may have even been Scottish, God help us. He wore blue not green, which we know from all the surviving artworks. Green was simply *not* Patrick's color. Nor did he drive the snakes out of Ireland. How do we know that? Well, because it's too cold here. No snake in their right mind would be setting up home in this place. And perhaps most surprising of all (now wait for this one), he isn't even actually a saint (in the Roman Catholic Church at least) as he has never been officially canonized as one.

So what exactly is a *saint*? And how precisely did they all of them get there in the first place? I mean they must be "mic-drop" holy, isn't that right? Or at least holier than the rest of us, which I appreciate for many mightn't be much of a competition, but bear with me on this. The Catholic Church has about ten thousand recognized saints due to a lot of papal fast-tracking in the Middle Ages as much as anything else. Regardless, a tidy number of men and women you'll agree, and it's based on a three-stage canonization process.

On the Reformed side of the house it's a bit different. It would have to be, wouldn't it? With us types, it can be a bit more "bottom-up." Saints are recognized in the first instance at the local level as a particular community remembers someone and begins to venerate that person. As time goes by, the veneration spreads and is adopted by other churches in other places. Eventually entire national churches sign on and officially recognize a saint, giving the saint his or her own feast day to be remembered throughout the church.

Regardless, both the Roman Catholic Church and other Christian churches tend to believe that saints, howsoever they have got there, have set the bar higher than the rest of us when it comes to godliness. Which does lead to a problem, however. If they are all so great, then what are the rest of us? Half as great? Not so great? Great enough but not that great? Maybe we are kind of the diluted version of saints? Perhaps a short anecdote might assist as we try to come to grips with what the rest of us might be.

For some time now I have had the privilege of working in hospital chaplaincy and, unsurprisingly, you get to see some things. Recently when I was on Sunday duty I met with a Christian lady in her early nineties. Let's call her Gillian. Bar a relatively minor issue she was, and is, in great fettle. A church stalwart all her life, if a Martian came down from space and asked you what a Christian lady in her nineties might look like, she was, and is, it. Kind, funny, and faithful notwithstanding that she could also kill a grown man at twenty paces.

Sometime later in the day in the emergency department I met Damien, a fifty-six-year-old life-long drug addict who had overdone it (again) on what he and his colleagues called "Zimos"—or more properly in pharmacy circles, Zimovane—a prescription sleeping pill. In Damien's case this time, about twenty of them. Damien, about six feet, four inches tall and equally wide, had a cry with me, said his life was a mess and so was he, and asked what had he done with it all. He also promised me he'd never *really* been in prison and had no outstanding warrants. Both of which I knew to be about as wide of the mark as could possibly be.

Cut to Monday morning and the Zimmerman himself, Damien, is pacing up and down outside the hospital. "John," he shouts, "I have to tell you about this lovely woman Gillian who's in the ward next to me. I think she's one of your lot." "She's lovely," he says. "A doll, and I've sat with her the last two days and had great fun with her. I make sure she has her rug over her feet and I turn off her side lamp for her in the evening."

It's worth thinking about for a moment. One person has spoken nicely to Damien and treated him kindly and he thinks he's just won the lottery. Gillian, too, is just doing what she always does, being nice to everyone, and she thinks nothing of it. Is Damien likely to reach the stages of "Venerable" or "Blessed" within the Vatican? I'm going to hazard a guess and say no. He is, after all, more likely to be canonized within the pharmaceutical industry than the church. Is Gillian going to achieve sainthood where she lives? Equally, almost certainly not. But Gillian and Damien have met in the most unlikely of circumstances and struck up a friendship that is meaningful for both. Different families, backgrounds, lives, and outlooks yet united by what they share: compassion and love.

You know, the broader Christian family doesn't get everything right. I can hear some of you say, John, it gets very little right; but on one matter some of its brethren may have just called the mark. We don't make individual saints. We say that all followers of Christ can be called saints. In which case I am going to nominate both Gillian and, yes, Damien as two modern-day saints I met—and I, for one, am not fit to tie the straps of their sandals. Because, you see, the feast of St. Patrick and all other saint feast days are all about the Gillians, just as much as they may be about the great man or woman for whom the days are named. They're all about the Damiens, just as much as it's about the majestic image we have of our numerous saints with their croziers.

Not all saints wear capes. Some of them, like Gillian, just have tartan rugs at the end of their beds or, for Damien, the latest in gray tracksuit bottoms. But they, dear reader, have more than many of us may have, for they show love from their heart and evidence compassion in their deeds. And you never know, if we can all try to practice these two things, maybe your neighborhood may soon even have a saint of its own.

Fancy the job?

You, Too, Are a Riot!

So Don't Condemn Others

You know I can't but be reminded of a well-known hymn of the Welsh valleys when I come to the last sentence in one passage of the Gospel from John when he talks about the eating of bread (John 6:51). And many of you will know this rousing Welsh hymn.

> Guide me, O Thou great Jehovah,
> Pilgrim through this barren land;
> I am weak, but Thou art mighty,
> Hold me with Thy pow'rful hand.
> Bread of heaven, Bread of heaven,
> Feed me till I want no more;
> Feed me till I want no more.[1]

The line from John's Gospel mentioned above chimes nicely with this. The one who eats this bread will live forever (John 6:51). So these are nice lines, in both the hymn and in John, right? But what do they actually mean? What bread exactly are we supposed to be feeding on? Well, it's not quite so complicated when we think about it for one moment. The bread we feed on is the bread of heaven. And what is that? Love. Love for Christ and, by implication, loving and feeling compassion for each other.

Well, I wonder, how are we all getting on with that? Well, for some of us, not too well if, following the horrific killing of three young girls in Liverpool, and the riotous events in recent years around Ireland and Britain are anything to go by. Nor are other jurisdictions immune. Least of all the US.

---

1. William Williams, "Guide Me, O Thou Great Jehovah," 1745, trans. Peter Williams, 1771.

You, Too, Are a Riot!

Yes, in recent years, there have been summers of discontent like few others across the British Isles and no one anywhere seems to truly know what prompted pensionable men and women, children to heap such misery and hatred on society. So if these street gladiators are politically ignorant, how do we explain these behaviors? It can't all be drink, or drugs, or just wanting a fight. Can it? Well, that can certainly be part of it but it doesn't go to its heart. What remains at the core of such behaviors is one word that underlies all our aggression, violence, and criminal behaviors, and that word is fear. Fear always trumps confidence. Confident men, boys, or women don't riot. You heard it here first. Let me explain.

One evening back in Dublin in 1975, as an eleven-year-old boy, I got the news over the kitchen table from my mother that two "lovely Germans" were moving in next door to us. They were both university lecturers, which almost gave her a seizure with the excitement. I remember my father however reacting like a nervous child in a fairground whose dad has just said they're going on that great (poorly maintained) roller coaster. Stunned didn't quite cover it.

I mean, how were we to behave beside Germans? After all, father was from County Waterford in rural Ireland and there wasn't much call for those German chaps there in the 1940s.

Soon my mother had invited them in for drinks, and I noticed—in a moment of mind-bending enthusiasm—my father had pulled his socks over the two legs of his brown suit before they arrived as a "mark of respect." "What *are* you doing?" my mother asked. "The German men wear their clothes like this," he replied, and he wasn't joking. "It'll make them feel at home," he asserted.

It was too late however for her to do anything. The doorbell went and my father, fearing an imminent assault from my mother, was now struggling to get the trouser legs out of both socks. Far worse, he was only partially successful. Quite what our Teutonic guests thought during the course of the evening as they stared at a man who looked like he had either only half got the lederhosen idea or was looking for his bike, or both, is anyone's guess. But I'm confident utterly bewildered wouldn't be a bad start.

You see my father had made a sincere if comedic attempt to welcome two Germans to our streets back in 1975, but even he was finding it all very stressful. Others take their "transition anxiety" to a new level and so, in Britain for example, some disaffected English felt it might be a good idea to riot against anyone who wasn't . . . emm . . . "properly them." Of course there remain granular "reasons" aplenty why we have had those riots, arson, and disorder across both countries and around the world.

These and other rioters of all ages have probably been the victims of any one or more of: zero parental attachment or warmth, no supervision, non-intact homes, social and economic deprivation, societal breakdown, labeling, shaming, social stigma, and learned behaviors. And believe me when I say, this is the tip of their melting iceberg. In reality the question is not, why were there so many people rioting across the country? It's, why weren't there *more*?

We can still blame them and on one level maybe we should; self-responsibility is after all something we all have to learn. However, its far easier to learn that lesson in a nice, comfortable family home where the world is set out before you like a king or queen than it is for others who are trampled on from birth, and often in their own homes before they have even stepped outside. The difficult truth for us is that as Christians when we are pointing the finger of blame, we had better be careful we notice the other three pointing back at us. What makes a lot of us better? Our accident of birth? Our education? Our money? All our advantages? Hardly. That is what actually makes us worse, for we remember in 2 Corinthians that the one who had much did not have *too* much, and the one who had little did not have *too* little (2 Cor 8:15).

Those rioters and arsonists feared change. They feared the transition that they believed they saw before them and they didn't care how they expressed it. Why would they? They have after all, in their eyes, nothing to lose. So the question for believers is not why rioters may have behaved so badly and in such a frightful way, or why there may or may not be too much or too little immigration. The question surely is, What can we do about the society we all share to ensure that such an expression of fear and hatred becomes our past?

And the answer remains within our gift, and that answer is love, compassion, and forgiveness for immigrants and insurgents alike. That's the true bread of heaven I talked about at the beginning by the way.

Indeed, maybe if we had all exhibited these bounteous expressions of God in the first place, we might be in a better place. Remember, Colossians tells us that we remain his chosen people, for we are holy and dearly loved, and so we must now clothe ourselves with compassion, kindness, humility, gentleness, and patience (Col 3:12). It has been said that courage does not always roar but rather, sometimes, it's the quiet voice at the end of the day saying, "I will try again tomorrow." As Christians, we must now hear that voice.

Memories Are Made of This
Time Fades, God Radiates

YOU KNOW, AS I was thinking about Pentecost this last while I couldn't help but notice one theme—that of consistency. This idea that Christ is always by our side in the form of the Holy Spirit and especially at times when we think he may be most absent. When we think about our own lives we might imagine for the most part that they have a pattern that we can predict. We go to school, we get a job, we find a partner if we are lucky, we have kids if we are very, very lucky, and maybe we even get to see their kids. And then we die and go to God. We hope.

The problem with our lives on this earth is that all things come and go, all the time. Let me give you some examples. What reader can remember when so many people smoked you almost had to apologize if you didn't light up a cigarette? Okay, don't all put your hands up at once. I mean, in those days it was legal to blow smoke in a baby's face and if it cried then you had a problem baby, not you. In fact, in some families, the baby might even have blown its own smoke back in your face. Those days have, thankfully, gone.

What about our dress sense? What was women's fascination with dustcoats in their homes back in the 1970s? My mother had a dustcoat for every occasion including one for when she was in a good mood or a bad mood. When women left the home (assuming they ever did), then on went the head scarf. Look at old TV reels from the 1960s and 1970s. There were no self-respecting women who would leave their homes without such a fashion statement, with the usual excuse, because "they had just got their hair done." When they came back into the house, off went the head scarf, on went the dustcoat, into the mouth went the cigarette, and the feet were then firmly positioned—where? That's right, Madam, on the linoleum. In

1970s Europe, "lino" was the drug of choice and we were all addicted. Those days have also gone.

When we went out for an evening we could find ourselves meeting anywhere. Theaters long since demolished. Ballrooms knocked down. Queuing around the corner to go to cinema. Meeting dates under various clocks, hoardings, and signs now also lost in the mist of time. Our favorite ads on TV? Now they all look really silly, and how we laugh. And for those with muscular memories, they're in the bin alongside *Dallas*, *Dynasty*, *Falcon Crest*, and *Knots Landing*; and, for the Brits, *Tomorrow's World* and *Top of the Pops*. All gone. In Ireland we even had an "agony aunt" radio show called *Dear Frankie* where Frankie once read out the most immortal of questions ever to be read out on such an agony aunt program: "Dear Frankie," said the female caller, "I've been going out with a man with a wooden leg. Should I break it off?" Yet Frankie is gone now, too.

And it's not just people or places that are gone. Some of our cultural habits and language have gone too. Mothers in Ireland back in the day, for example, would proudly announce they were "doing the messages." Not going to the shops, mind you. No, they were "doing the messages." Whatever the messages were. Nor did we get depressed in those days. Oh no. We were either "having a lie down" or, sometimes when things got bad, we might "take to the bed." I had an uncle who had social anxiety, drank too much, and had an odd fascination with Ford Capris. He wasn't in need of mental health intervention. Not a bit of it. He simply "suffered from his nerves."

Speaking of which, my nerves weren't great either. I can remember my parents getting central heating installed in our big, old, red brick house and my mother saying to me that if I ever had the temerity to turn it on, she would not be responsible for her actions. There was a similar horror on the faces of the mothers of Ireland if you went within five feet of the button on the immersion, which if pressed, would almost certainly end up in a nuclear holocaust for the whole country. Immersions had after all only one real rival on the blowing-the-house-up front—that's right—pressure cookers.

For better or for worse, all that language and those primeval fears are now gone too. So everything comes and goes and, as Eccl 1:2 says, everything in life can seem "meaningless"—the Hebrew word used is *hebel*—because nothing, and I mean nothing, lasts in our lives. Including our own. Which is a depressing idea. Unless of course we have found Christ and that one word, love. And God's love for us is everywhere in Scripture. Acts, for example, tells us that the coming of the Lord will be a great and glorious day and everyone who calls on the name of the Lord will be saved (Acts 2:21). Romans advises that the Spirit of the Lord will helps us in our weakness when Jesus is gone (Rom 8:26). John's Gospel, that when the Holy Spirt comes he will guide us all in truth, the truth that is God's love for us (John 16:13).

Because you see, long after *Magnum, P.I.* and *Murder, She Wrote* have left our screens and the last dustcoat has been folded away one final time in the well-loved "hot press," and well after the echoes of our mothers' voices, telling us as kids that we will catch pneumonia if go out in the rain, have all, too, drifted off into the mist of time, we are left with one glorious truth. God the Father, God the Son, and, especially today and always, God the Holy Spirit will never leave us for he loved us not only since the beginning of time but will love us until the end. Indeed, if we were in any doubt, he has already inscribed us into the palms of his hands and, as he says, our walls are ever before him (Isa 49:16).

And so when there are times when we hanker after the old days and the totems of our young lives, try not to dwell in the sadness but the happiness of those days we had, and which were given us by Christ. And when we worry that we cannot find the Christ who graced us with so much, maybe try not to worry too much, because we know from Scripture that his Holy Spirit will always find us in the luminous darkness of our lives. Indeed, God promises us across Scripture that when he left this earth in human form he would send his Holy Spirit to us; and so he has never left us.

In truth, when he appears most absent he is actually never more present.

Perspective Is Everything
Don't Sweat—God Doesn't

WELL, IT'S BEEN A busy past couple of years in the news and so I'm not going to pull any punches. So buckle up everyone; this promises to be a roller-coaster ride. You see, we have all been getting *very* animated about news "stuff." Some of it is, in fairness, very serious. Our interest ebbs and flows regarding Ukraine and the Middle East generally, and other tragedy soaked events can, at times, engage us more. For example, we became especially interested in the lives of those poor five souls who lost their lives in recent years diving in a capsule to view the *Titanic*. We began to know something of their backgrounds, which were privileged to say the least, and we found that all very interesting. After all, we like privileged.

This news also played into our deepest fear of being trapped in a confined space if we knew our time was up. Could we think of anything worse? Hardly. How would we react? How would we feel? What if we were in that capsule with our son or daughter? Oh, and the five people actually in the capsule? Yes, that must have been terrible for them, too . . .

And then on other occasions, we go to other "tragedies." We are all horrified, for example, at the lack of corporate governance in public institutions in which we are all now experts. Forget global warming, famine, disease, or poverty; this appears to be the real news, ladies and gentlemen. For example, members of the European Parliament (MEPs) collectively earn more than €8.6 million a year from outside jobs.[1] This also comes from private companies that actively lobby on EU policy according to a report published by Transparency International EU in 2024. In some cases, these

---

1. Jack Schickler, "Revealed: MEPs' Millions in Outside Earnings," *Euronews*, May 6, 2024, www.euronews.com/my-europe/2024/05/06/revealed-meps-millions-in-outside-earnings.

Perspective Is Everything

parliamentarians earn more from outside activities than they do from their MEP salary of €10,000 a month. In the US things are no better. The CEO of Carlyle Group earned $187 million per annum while Jon Winkelried, CEO of TPG, almost managed to bag $200 million for a year's salary. Nice work if you can get it, and, yes, we were very interested in that.

So let's all discuss these things. A lot. Because this is really, really important stuff. Of course we all know it's not. Or do we? Not that the loss of those five lives on that capsule was not a tragic event. It was. Utterly. But what about when it's a story about migrants on boats? Where was the global chat about that ship that sank with migrants off the coast of Greece? The Messenia migrant boat disaster, which sank about fifty miles of the coastal town of Pylos in Greece. Not five souls, by the way. In fact, the UN says between 400 and 750 people could have been crammed onto the vessel.[2]

In fact, this may be the worst migrant boat disaster, ever. How many of us, I wonder, put ourselves into the position of the eighteen-year-old Pakistani boy or the Syrian man in that vessel who were thrown from that boat in the dead of night amid the screaming and death cries? People who would have certainly suffered a horrendous last few moments as their lives flashed before them. Why did they not get the same mental airplay, I wonder, as the occupants of the *Titan* capsule at the time? After all, we grieved ever so enthusiastically when it came to those unfortunate individuals. Could that all really have been about us imagining such a horror befalling ourselves?

In fact, if we were truly honest, it's even worse than that. I can guarantee you that all of us here reading this today have given more thought to certain CEOs' and celebrities' income than the Greek migrant-boat horror. Guaranteed. I mean, are we all having a laugh? And, by the way, I most certainly include myself in all of this.

For the avoidance of any doubt, we need to start reminding ourselves of some home truths when it comes to who we all really are. We love advising each other that we are made in God's image. Well if we are, we might need to give that mirror a bit of a wipe. Why don't we try with Matt 10 for starters? It doesn't pull any punches: "A disciple is not above the teacher, nor a slave above the master" (10:24). You and I are no better, or no worse, than the hundreds of souls who lost their lives near Greece or, indeed, the five men who died in that capsule. We are neither above or below them, nor they us. How do we know this? Because remember, as Matthew's Gospel

---

2. BBC, "Greece Boat Disaster: 350 Pakistanis Were On Board, Minister Says," June 23, 2023, www.bbc.com/news/world-asia-65997635.

reminds us in that same passage of Scripture, not one of those sparrows will fall to the ground unperceived by our Father (Matt 10:29). Remember, the hairs on the heads of these migrants were all counted too. Yet these are the people that you and I have relegated behind those whose lives we think (without ever admitting) might be more valuable, or more interesting, or more relatable than that of a Pakistani boy, or a Syrian man.

And just in case we have still not got the message, Jesus says to us in Matt 10:37 that, "Whoever loves father or mother more than me, is not worthy of me; and whoever loves son or daughter more than me is not worthy of me." I wonder what Jesus would say about all of us, therefore, these last few years, and who we appear to "love." We, his Christian people, who valued the *Titan* capsule story, where five lives were lost, above the sinking of the migrant boat near Greece, where between 500 and 700 people may have perished.[3] We, his Christian people, who are genuinely more captivated by the newsworthiness of a chat show host's or actor's salary than the slaughter of innocents in any number of war-torn areas of the world. Have we all lost the run of ourselves? The answer, of course, is yes. But the message of Christ remains firmly anchored in Matthew. "Whoever does not take up the cross and follow me is not worthy of me," says Christ. "Those who find their life will lose it, and those who lose their life for my sake will find it" (Matt 10:38–39).

The time for all believers patting themselves on the back about how they go about their safe, middle-income, so-called middle-class version of Christianity needs to end. Following Christ really should be messy, unsatisfactory, and mostly, wholly uncomfortable. If it's not, we simply are not doing it right. Now let us *really* take up our crosses and follow him by genuinely remembering equally all those who perished in Greece, as well as on that capsule.

You can even remember actors and CEOs too, if you want, in your prayers. But you know what? Try not to forget any other soul in the process.

---

3. Wikipedia, "2023 Messenia Migrant Boat Disaster," last modified Nov. 16, 2024, https://en.wikipedia.org/w/index.php?title=2023_Messenia_migrant_boat_disaster&oldid=1257747810.

For the Love of God
Give Him a Chance

When I've talked about the passion of Christ in the past, I've seen people immediately move into a medical coma. "Passion" and "Christ" just don't seem to work together for the modern reader, and somehow it feels somewhat "yesterday" to even talk about the passion of Christ. That's assuming we even truly know what it means. So let's try to look at the passion of Christ in a somewhat different way. Firstly, let us try to remember what words *actually* mean. For example, I think my generation, and possibly one or two before mine, may have been the expert generations in speaking in sentences and words that we all used, but never really considered.

For instance, I wonder who of you here tonight remembers something along the lines of this from their mother. "I am going to kill you," my mother would say to me when I had done something I shouldn't have done, which was just about every day. In fairness to her she never carried out that threat or came near to it, but I wasn't a man to test her. Nonetheless, I knew I could substitute the words "get very angry, then calm down, then give you a cuddle" for "kill."

You see, words have a habit of losing their meaning, drifting off from generation to generation, becoming a watered-down option, if you will. *Love*, of course, is our classic example. Time was, that love was a deep, meaningful if not spiritual bond between two people. That was it. Nowadays, however, it's perfectly acceptable to love everything—from a Big Mac to our favorite pair of socks—and no one bats an eyelid. "Oh, my gawd," the young people cry, "I just love your latest Instagram post. Totes emosh." Last night I heard one of my college-going daughters describe a friend as someone she "*actually* really loved." "Oh, was that Hazel from primary school?" I asked. "Whom you have known since?" "No, it's this totes amazing girl I met last week at work," she says. "I just love her. If anything happened to her, I don't know what I'd do." I and her mother were too busy picking our jaws up off the floor to respond.

You see, in the land of the young people, and sometimes a few older ones too, it is of course possible to love everyone, and everything, always, except with one caveat. Not really. As that exceptionally niche British-American rock band of the 1980s Foreigner once famously sang, "I want to know what love is." Well, you and me both, Mr. Foreigner. So words are very important, and of course how we use them. And Scripture, time and time again, contains classic examples of that word that we have all heard before—a word we overuse, underuse, misuse, and generally squeeze the linguistic lights out of. And that word is of course *love*—occasionally confused with passion. The problem is that we are all so busy either loving everyone and everything equally (or hating them for that matter, but that is another discussion) that many of us still haven't still quite grasped its proper meaning.

So let's try and get this word in context once and for all this evening. Firstly, it's a very big word—in fact, it doesn't get any bigger. Now you might say to me, John, there is something bigger than love—how about the universe for a start? True. The universe is about 13.7 billion years old. I repeat, 13.7 billion years old; that's a long time to be shuffling around. But wait. It could be far, far older than that. Our big bang could have been preceded by millions of other big bangs, a concept loosely known as the inflationary multiverse.[1] Which can also mean that we may extrapolate and suggest there was no beginning to time, and the universe may have *always* been here. Wrap your heads around that one, Madam. Fair enough, the universe is pretty big. But some time back, little old me, Marmite man, with his baldie head and his extraordinary nose had a "roundy" birthday. And to "celebrate" I went with all my family to see a local soccer team play on that night. I know, I hear you. Be still my beating heart. And while God may not have been with my team on the particular evening, love was there as I sat there with my variously interested five children and wife.

And you see, it's this type of comically ordinary stuff that marks our lives. The ones that really matter and show that word *love*, maybe more than the inflationary universe can ever do. Our little birthdays, events, families,

---

1. Ethan Siegel, "The Strongest Evidence for a Universe Before the Big Bang," Starts with a Bang, *Big Think*, Mar. 16, 2023, https://bigthink.com/starts-with-a-bang/evidence-universe-before-big-bang.

and our lives matter, not just to you and I, of course, but to God. In fact, they matter more than we can ever know in our human form. They matter in ways that we cannot ever begin to understand. Because there is one thing bigger than the billions and trillions of planets, stars, and galaxies. There is one thing bigger than time and space; there is one thing bigger than it all, and that is God. And what else? That's right; his love for you and me so beautifully expressed in John's Gospel at Easter week in Christ's faith, his suffering, and his forgiveness.

You know, Vladimir Nabokov may have struck a chord when he once said, "our existence is but a brief crack of light between two eternities of darkness."[2] Yet *what* a nanosecond it is! So by all means engage with the big stuff—cosmology and astrophysics—as Christ would have wanted, for it is indeed an awesome area. Too awesome for our heads, truth be told. But when you have finished grappling with the first and second laws of thermodynamics, don't be surprised if you are suddenly afraid. Very afraid. It is after all simply too much for us to comprehend, and that which we cannot understand makes us fearful. But we need not be, ever. Hear the simple words instead of John 13:34–35 ringing in our ears: "Love one another. Just as I have loved you, you also should love one another. By this everyone will know that you are my disciples." The meaning of the passion of Christ, you see, was there all along, hiding in full view, right in front of us, and it was love, for all other anchors of our faith flow through and out of it.

The truth is that when all the "roundy" birthdays are over, and when all those trillions and zillions of galaxies, planets, and stars have packed up and turned their lights off for the last time, Christ will welcome us, for he has a place prepared for you all, for me, for everybody. So let the young people misuse the word *love* in whatever way they wish. That is their job as young people. They'll get it. Eventually. From now on, love yourself, love each other, and love God. For *that*, ladies and gentlemen, is the true passion of the Christ—one that we may have sometimes missed in the past.

So no more excuses, and remember . . . keep on lovin' as Christ loves us.

---

2. Vladimir Nabokov, *Speak, Memory: An Autobiography Revisited* (London: Penguin Classics, 2000), chap. 1.

The Nothing People
Nothing Comes from Nothing—Ask God

Us religious types all say we have faith in God. That is why we go to church every Sunday, John, I hear my congregation say to me. Now move along with the other stuff, like a good minister. Yet one Gospel passage brings us right back into the center of the topic and we smile as we normally do at that old favorite, the doubting Thomas in John 20:24.

I mean, how could he be so naïve? That would certainly not be us, we say. We cannot understand (through the comfort of our warm, Western world lenses over two thousand years later) how Thomas could have been so skeptical. I mean, wasn't it obvious we all say to ourselves? We would definitely have believed without having to see the mark of the nails in Jesus' hand and in his side. Thomas was a nice scriptural creature we say, but, between us all, something of a biblical joke. I mean, imagine not believing. Ha! That's mad, we say. It's probably at this point that we should pause for breath as we trot out the same old lines to ourselves and others about Thomas. The truth is not only are we all like Thomas, we are all exactly like Thomas, probably worse, day in and day out. The reality is that many of us can come across a YouTube clip created by some over-confident twenty-two-year-old nonbeliever in California, and our lifetime faith in God can then suffer far more than a speed wobble.

The seemingly random nature of the universe and our planet and the terrible things that happen to its inhabitants, especially our friends and family (though other people's sufferings are available), can send us into a Richard Dawkins-like atheistic spiral. The smallest thing on any given day can and does test whatever belief we may think we have in God and his love for us. For me it started when I was much younger. I remember my father saying to me one December, "John, it's time I told you. There is

The Nothing People

no Santa Claus. It's all entirely make believe. It's myself and your mother putting those presents under the tree each Christmas." Well you can only imagine my little world fell apart. I had placed faith not only in Santa Claus but also in my father, that he too believed in him. Now in a few seconds he shattered all my dreams in pieces on the floor. My father said subsequently that his heart was in the right place when he told me that day, but, as you can imagine, it was still a bitter pill for me to swallow as an enthusiastic twenty-five-year-old.

So, if we are being truly honest with ourselves, nonbelievers don't help us in our journey to God, now do they? Let's have a look at them. In the red corner, we have a group called, for want of a better term, the "old atheists." That means they were a bit politer than the newer ones.

In any event, as far back as Epicurus, we were given this atheistic riddle:

> Is God willing to prevent evil, but not able?
> Then he is not omnipotent.
> Is he able, but not willing?
> Then he is malevolent.
> Is he both able and willing?
> So why the evil?
> Is he neither able or willing?
> Then why call him God?[1]

Then came to the so-called New Atheists, the doubting Thomases par excellence, but this time in laced-up boots. I am specifically thinking of the Four Horsemen, as they are described, of New Atheism, namely, Richard Dawkins, Sam Harris, Daniel Dennett, and Christopher Hitchens. God knows what poor old biblical Thomas would have done if confronted by these new-corner boys of militant atheism. I mean Thomas wasn't even able to believe when he was surrounded by believers—and Christ himself!

So today there is no dispute that not to be a doubting Thomas is very difficult. We live in a world where everyone wants 100 percent empirical research evidence for anything that may be said (provided they don't have to provide it, of course), and so us believers appear to be lost in the secular desert. After all, it's much easier to laugh at the idea of a bearded man up in the sky who we are all going to be with on an eternal play date when we die, than it is to engage in theological debate about intelligent design and inflationary cosmology.

---

1. See David Hume, *Dialogues Concerning Natural Religion*, ed. Martin Bell (1779; repr., London: Penguin Classics, 1990), 94–104.

Part 1: Reflections from the Shadows

But let's give it some thought here now though, shall we? And with grateful thanks to young, Christian US comedian Pete Holmes, I am now going to borrow a wonderfully accurate comedy sketch from his show *I Am Not for Everyone* to explain.

> Some people [that would be us by the way, Madam] think God created the universe. Some people think *nothing* created the universe. Which is the funniest guess? And the nothing people make fun of the God people. They say God doesn't exist. I'm like, okay, maybe . . . But you know what *definitely* doesn't exist? *Nothing*. That's the defining characteristic of nothing, is that it doesn't exist.
>
> So what are we talking about? Either you think its God, something you can't see, touch, taste, photograph, and science can't prove, or you think it's nothing. Something you can't see, touch, taste, photograph, and science can't prove. But I think we can all agree, if nothing, if your nothing, sometimes spontaneously erupts into everything, that's a pretty [expletive], magical, [expletive] *nothing* you guys. And ask, ask the *nothing* people, What happens when you die? They'll tell you, Nothing. You go into *nothing*. I'm like, you mean you merge back with your creator? That's heaven![2]

Pete Holmes, take a bow. You have managed to encapsulate in two paragraphs what Christian apologists have been trying to do for two millennia. Which brings me full circle back to that word faith and our doubting Thomas. Like Thomas, the young people (and the not so young, incidentally) love that word *evidence*, and I mean they really love it. And they really think that everything they do in their lives is 100 percent evidence-based. So you ask them, Are you 100 percent sure that when you go home this evening that your older sister won't put some poison in your dinner? And they'll laugh and say, well, they are pretty sure from the evidence of experience with her that won't happen.

Then I say, Oh right, and ask them, When you go to the pharmacist's for your next prescription, I assume you will go in there with your chemistry testing kit? And they say, No John, Why would I? And I say, Well, after all, can you be 100 percent certain that the chemist isn't having an off day and won't either intentionally or mistakenly give you the wrong prescription? And the young people will laugh, and smile knowingly, and say, Of course not, as they have "confidence" from previous experiences that won't happen. So I say to them, Oh, so you have "faith" that it won't happen, in

---

2. Pete Holmes, *I Am Not for Everyone*, directed by Oren Brimer (Netflix, 2023), at 50:02.

The Nothing People

the same way that others have faith in a God that exists outside space, time, and matter, based on your lived experience and evidence?

And they say to me, No John, that is not the same thing. We have *confidence*, they say, not faith. And, of course, because they are young people they know no Latin. So I tell them that *confidence* comes from the Latin word *confidentia*, which, I say, guess what, means to have an intensive trust or faith in something. "Awks," as those young people might say.

You see we can all be doubting Thomases during our lives, and we will be, and that is okay, and Jesus knows that. I mean, why do you think we have it in Scripture? Despite the noise though around you, pay heed all you doubting Thomases out there, that as a matter of philosophical, theological, and scientific observation and discovery, we have far more evidence for the existence of our loving God than against.

But you can all look at that in your own time. The greatest evidence of all? Love. And those who do not love, cannot know God. And why? Because God is love. So no more excuses. And remember, don't worry about Pete Holmes's "nothing" people. God loves them as much as he loves us. But never forget: we are the "something" people, and for that reason we are most blessed, for that is our faith.

Annie's Song

God Is Love and So Are Mothers

The problem with Scripture is, well... there is so much to preach about. I often feel as confused as when an Englishman places three shovels up against the wall and then asks an Irishman to take his pick. (I'm Irish by the way. Only I can say that one.) But one line did come back to me again and again on the train today. And that is from Exodus; that one simple commandment: "Honour your father and your mother" (20:12). Of course it's a wonderful idea, although we might change the word to "respect" today and the rest would probably look after itself. We can after all learn a lot from our parents, good and bad, but having respect for them when we have them isn't a bad start. And dare I say to all parents and grandparents out there, having respect for our children and grandchildren isn't a bad idea either.

Now I don't know about you, but whatever way I shake up that commandment I tend to focus on honoring your mother most especially. This doesn't mean Dad doesn't count, of course, but sure, look, he'll probably be fine either way, and there's nothing a visit to the pub or a round of golf won't cure in any event. But Mother? Well, she's an altogether different kettle of fish. Then I thought to myself, in a way, every Sunday is mothering Sunday, and mothers are worth it. We can talk about them every day if they want. So, if you like, treat this as the warm-up act to the proper sermon you will presumably get on next Mother's Day when, of course, it's going to be mother central everywhere. Today, however, as you pour your first glass of red, we may have time for a little more mature refection outside the noise of that day.

Mothering Sunday can of course evoke a myriad of feelings in us all. For those of us lucky enough to still have ours with us, the day is spent allegedly mothering them for a change. For those of us not so lucky, perhaps many of us reading this, it's all about the memories. You see, mothers have a habit of doing what it says on the tin without anyone noticing and we can get very used to that. One thing we can all agree on, however, is that mothers are, as they say in the media, "across" everything. In truth, you would want to get up very early in the morning to catch your average mother out. And, incidentally, on occasions when you do? She doesn't like it.

But do we really understand how important our mothers are to our psychological and spiritual well-being, or, indeed, lack of it? Without wishing to get too technical, do we ever give a moment to consider how important a mother's love is in ensuring we don't, for example, as my own late mother would say, turn out to be a half-fool? Of course the answer is no. Mothers are considered by many to be simply a benevolent figure in our lives, hovering just above the ground in their luminous dustcoats. While they may have an influence on who we become as people, some of us still believe that their effect is important but not critical.

Incorrect. We know from research that children require continuous and consistent caregiving to the age of five and absence of this will have harmful psychological, and possibly criminal, consequences for them in later life.[1] Importantly though, we equally know that separation is not the same as deprivation. You see, mothers work in mysterious ways, and let them at it, I say. After all, a mother can single-handedly turn a child's fortunes around notwithstanding the absence of another parental figure—Dad. As Proverbs advises us, mothers are clothed with strength and dignity and only they can truly laugh at the days to come (31:25).

Mothers are Mary of Nazareth, Mary Magdalene, and Ruth the Moabite all rolled into one. Yet when they are physically and/or emotionally absent from their child the psychological outcomes for that offspring as they grow into adulthood can never be underestimated. For not all mothers are necessarily glorious treasures, and many can be as broken as the rest of humanity. In reality, mothering Sunday is every bit as much about them as it is about the mothering exemplars of Christ's love. You see, some mothers do forget their children; they abandon them, and they can leave them on psychological scrap heaps, keeping therapists, and indeed criminal defense lawyers, busy up and down the country.

The reality is that for the bulk of us our mothers probably fall somewhere in the middle of all our chat about them. Neither exceptional nor

---

1. Saul McLeod, "John Bowlby's Attachment Theory," Simply Psychology, Jan. 24, 2024, www.simplypsychology.org/bowlby.html.

Part 1: Reflections from the Shadows

unexceptional, their parenting would be characterized in popular psychological verbiage as "good enough." Yet "good enough" mothering is not as pedestrian as it seems. In fact, it is quite the opposite.

Annie Deane-O'Keeffe, my mother, was one such mother, and she was, just like yours I imagine, not without her failings. Yet on November 12, 2020, this giving woman who, when not nursing appeared anchored into my well-being for my entire life, passed to Christ, leaving one simple legacy.

That may have been the day my life went from color to black-and-white, but with one very good reason. She, like many mothers, had given a lifetime of unconditional love and compassion for her two children and for all those she met and, indeed, did not meet. So think about this on every mother's big day, and your own mother's birthday. Just like your mothers, my mother loved and was loved. I like to call it "Annie's Song" in her memory. Every day as Christians we must realize that it must be the song that we sing for all our mothers. And always remember that, as her son or daughter, she was your first love, and in many ways she will also be your last.

So as we think about the fourth commandment of Exodus and whether we did or did not honor our parents, and especially our mothers, we happily remind ourselves of the words used in "Annie's Song" by John Denver (you should look up the lyrics!), as we pray to the God who now holds some of them in his arms.

Putin the Terrible
Hard to Love, Easy to Hate

YOU KNOW, I COULD stand up on any given Sunday and talk about one thing, and one thing alone. Whatever the reading, whatever the Gospel, one word shines through all the darkness as we try to follow Christ. That word? Love. I don't need to remind you that *love* has been somewhat diluted in recent times. Everyone appears to *love* everyone and everything from something as profound as their spouse to a large bar of chocolate. Today, love is an infinite spectrum. Indeed, the poor word has arguably become so meaningless it really could do with a bit of counseling. But we are Christians, so apparently we have a better handle on the word than some. Regardless, let's be careful where we see the word in the Bible, and, yet think we *do not* see it.

For example, in parts of 1 Corinthians you may be forgiven for thinking that it is often just about how the Lord is really quite unfair, he's not listening to us, and there we all are, suffering to beat the band. And, for sure, that is part of it. Yet the prophet advises us that the answer is that we need to be patient while we wait for Christ to come to our aid. As a reminder, what is love, according to 1 Corinthians? That's right—it is patient (1 Cor 13:4). To remind us further, let us remember this verse from 1 Cor 13:13 again: "And now these three remain: faith, hope and love. But the greatest of these is love" (NIV). You see? You can't have one, with the other; faith without love.

Okay. So that is nice and easy and we get the idea that the Bible is essentially a book of love and, sure, all we need to do is love everyone and we will all be fine. Couldn't be easier, right? But wait, we have a problem. While we are Christians, some of our fellow human beings are simply hard to love. There. I've said it. We all know it; we have all felt it at one time or

Part 1: Reflections from the Shadows

another, and there is no getting away from it. As hard as we may try, we will encounter people in our lives who appear almost medically unlovable. Others we will never encounter but still detest from afar for their despicable acts. They are bad; we are good. Fine. That was easy enough. Of course the problem is that we are all quite capable of being the "unlovable" at various points in *our* lives. Indeed, shame on you if you have not. Yet what of those people who really do push the boundaries by any measure of what we may call a minimum standard of human behavior? Those who murder, assault, rob, and engage in horrific acts of violence? What about those who may murder a son, a daughter, or indeed an entire family? Seriously? Can God really expect us to *love* them?

In my professional capacity, I have met these persons—and a lot of them—both in and outside prison. Tom was one such person I encountered some time back while doing research in an institution in the southeast of England. Jailed for life for a double murder and a range of offenses against children, he was every bit as repellent in person as were his incomprehensible acts. He was narcissistic, glib yet superficially charming; he had a comically grandiose sense of self-worth, was manipulative in discussion, and evidenced an utter lack of remorse, guilt, or empathy for any of his criminal acts. Coupled with his impulsivity, poor behavioral controls, and an excessive need for stimulation, Tom ticked each and every box for the personality disorder of them all—antisocial personality disorder. Without putting too fine a point on it, Tom was a psychopath.

Indeed, barring an implausible Pauline turnaround on the road to Damascus, Tom will likely die as he lived, an unrepentant and unremorseful psychopath. You see, he has made terrible choices for others, and yet these will have been calculated and laden with choice. We know this because he has, however, made, and will continue to make, what he will see as fantastic decisions for his own benefit. Feel sorry for him if you will, but Tom is assembling knowing choices all the day long.

Let's get even more focused. Take Vladimir Putin. Seriously. Can God really expect us to *love* him? Take just one, and I mean just one, example of how low his humanity can seemingly sink. His massacre at Mariupol in Ukraine (among many others) may be one of the worst twenty-first-century war crimes. It is estimated that some twenty thousand people were killed in this Putanic slaughter as it has become known. This is twice the number of deaths recorded in the entire two-year Nazi occupation of the city during World War II.[1] Indeed, barring an implausible turnabout on the road to Damascus, Vladimir Putin will probably die as he lived, an unrepentant and unremorseful dictator who is attempting to wipe a generation of humans out of history. It gets worse. These terrible choices *he* has made for others, all of which have been calculated and laden with choice. We know this because he has made, and will continue to make, what he will see as fantastic decisions for him and his own circle's benefit. Vladimir Putin appears to be assembling knowing choices all the day long.

Yet while there may be little or nothing we can do about *who* Putin or Tom are, there is quite a lot we, as Christians, can do about how we *feel* about them. We can be angry, very angry with them, and that is okay. If you don't believe me (and with grateful thanks to the New Testament), think flipping tables in the temple (Matt 21:12) and anger regarding the treatment of children (Mark 10:14) to name but two biblical eruptions. But we have a serious challenge as Christians. I, like you, have zero difficulty loving my children and, indeed, my late parents. Other family, kind friends, colleagues from past and present? All of them will get a grade of adoration from yours truly. Somewhere between one and ten on the love barometer. Lucky them. The problem is that on the *love* front, individuals like Vladmir Putin down through the ages present much greater challenges, however. In fact, it really doesn't get more difficult. Can we *love* him or truly feel compassion for him, as we normally understand the word? Ever? Perhaps not. But truthfully, though, I am not sure even Christ might fault any of us too much for that.

Here's the bit we cannot avoid, however. We can and indeed must love Vladimir Putin's human existence; the simple fact that he is made in God's image, absent any of his indescribable conduct. You see, we can legislate for our own behavior, and in the final Christian analysis there is no easy way to say this: Putin and his ilk were, and always will be, the gold standard for our love and compassion. Not our families, friends, or those we find easy to love. Love Vladimir Putin, and we see the face of God; despise him, and we continue our search.

No one ever said this Christian thing was easy.

---

1. Paul Niland, "Putin's Mariupol Massacre Is One of the 21st Century's Worst War Crimes," *UkraineAlert* (blog), Atlantic Council, May 24, 2022, www.atlanticcouncil.org/blogs/ukrainealert/putins-mariupol-massacre-is-one-the-worst-war-crimes-of-the-21st-century.

I Believe!
Or Do I . . .

I WAS SPEAKING TO A friend of mine the other day and we got to talking about life, death, and the universe, as you do. I asked him if he was a religious man to which came the standard reply, "Not really; I'm more spiritual." What did he actually mean by *spiritual*? I asked. "Well, we don't go to church," he said. This is a common condition across the Western world and beyond. Believers of whatever faith appear to have herded themselves into a new station, *spirituality*. Destination? Whatever you're having yourself. And of course that's okay because this is kind of how we now all roll. "Don't pin me down, Baby Jesus," we say. "I'll catch you later, but right now I've got to go to Walmart/Sainsbury's/Tesco. I'll think about you when I'm on the snack and chip aisle getting my peanut butter and jelly. Promise."

More institutionally, however, it appears that God has taken something of a back seat in recent years only to be replaced by a diluted version of himself. The *spirituality* version is impressively nebulous, so defying any real description or definition. None of us, after all, want to marked down as a bit of a religious fool who may still wear cheesecloth shirts and corduroy underwear, and so this is a good descriptor on which to hedge our bets. Put simply, if the God of the Old Testament were a fashion item today, he would have the same street cachet as a pair of dungarees or clogs. Think Walton Mountain for older readers.

So where did the God, of either the Old or the New Testament, go? Presumably he can move fairly freely within restricted boundaries and even across borders, whether we build a wall or not. In fact, more than ever, chances are he's probably still hanging around homes, supermarkets, roads, airports, and hoods, not to mention a few police stations. Yet getting an appointment with your family doctor would be easier. Your rector or pastor or priest keeps telling you that God is available twenty-four seven, and all you have to do is ask and he will come to you, and yet that hasn't worked. In fact, in the world in which we all live, he has never seemed so far away to many. So whose fault is that?

Well, in fairness, you could blame God. After all you asked for a meeting and he never arrived. And, in any event, does he even exist you say. I mean, c'mon. Churches are run by self-serving humans (always a problem, and of which more later) and your minister appears more interested in golf than the afterlife. And that's not even mentioning the small matter of world disasters, famines, hunger, and pestilence. God? He's a funny guy. Never there when you need him—and that's assuming for some that he's even there at all. Now when it comes to sitting easy with this blame game, some of you reading this may in a better place than others. Some of you may have been struck by the metaphorical bolt of biblical lightning during your lives, and this is to be envied. One minute you are as a secular as a Megan Thee Stallion (ask your children/grandchildren), the next you are front and center at the foot of the cross and all is very, and I mean very, clear.

For many, though, their relationship with God will at times seem like walking through wet concrete. No epiphanies, no revelations, and often no real sense of any promised land. To give us our due, folk like us did sort of look for him all our lives, but we could not seem to really find him. We gave him a knowing nod at births, weddings, and funerals, but then we moved on. We are busy after all, and, look, he must be up to his eyes also. Yes, there were other times we took a peak in various nooks and crannies in our lives, but still nothing. Others of us tried over and over again to find him out in a type of "hide-and-seek lite" yet still he evaded us. Some bargained with him, others hedged their bets with him, while a few of us may even have tried to bully him. Still nothing. God, our God, why did you forsake us?

Yet there he was, all along, hiding in plain sight. While we were taking the road less traveled he was on the superhighway waiting for us and all we had to do was to pay the odd toll. The truth was he had never gone away albeit we may have. You see, the time to meet God is not when we have won the lottery or gotten that new job. He's happy enough to take a back seat in those times and let us off with ourselves. After all, we will run ourselves out. We always do. No, the time to find him is now and the place may even be here, today, wherever we are. In our darkest hour we all may truly discover him and he will appear to us, as if from nowhere. We all know that as we hold the hand of a dying father, mother, brother, or sister he can never seem as real. Remember the bolt of lightning we thought missed some of us? We were wrong. It hit us a long time back when we felt indescribable love for our family, a friend, a stranger. That was him and, yes, Sunday school wasn't all wrong.

He who loves, knows God, therefore God will always reside in him. Some see him more than most. Those on the frontline and in law enforcement for sure. In the final moments of lives lost on our roads, by a school shooter, in tragedies, and in hospitals, in their last hours it may be others with them when we, their families, cannot be. It is at these times that they and we may feel his presence—or, not at all. This is, after all, the human condition—choice—and there will surely never be a better time to choose, for choose we must. Put simply, the God of Abraham says that when at our worst, we are in fact at our best. It is in our blackest hour that he may shine forth in that luminous darkness. Whomever we worship, God, Allah, YHWH, Vishnu, or any variety of same, he never, of course, went away, albeit we may have. Certainly nonbelief can be a settled position provided it has been considered thoroughly throughout life, as with those of faith who assert *their* belief. And yes, even "spiritualists" have their place, provided the label has real meaning for them.

Regardless, from these incomprehensible times in which we now live, many of us will emerge as perhaps the best equipped of all of to lead. And the ones where Christ always resides? The ones who are the most difficult to love or accept. The despised. The rapists, the child molesters, and the clergy who do such things. For the truth may be if God is love, then these could be a very special places where he resides. After all, any of us can love our families, that's the easy one. But our enemies? Those who commit the worst crimes imaginable toward children, sometimes while wearing a clerical collar? How can we possible love them?

We have much to learn from them, but once we find a place in our hearts for them we begin to find him. "Love your enemies and pray for those who persecute you," says Matt 5:44. No one ever said this belief stuff was easy but, finally, always remember that on those days you simply don't believe in him because of witnessing some of life's most terrible injustices laid before you, don't worry about it. He, after all, always believes in you.

The Evil Within
Closer Than We Think

You know, I often get struck in Scripture by many things, but one word especially always jumps out and startles me. The word? *Evil*. In John's Gospel, for example, Jesus at one point is asking God to protect his disciples after his departure from this earth against what he describes as "the evil one" (John 17:15). We assume here he means Satan and all the usual demonic forces that follow him around. It's a big descriptor to use against anyone but, in fairness, if any person can use it we might all agree that Jesus himself has a special dispensation in this regard. Yet it's a word we all use very glibly nowadays, against anyone or anything that doesn't quite fit into what we regard as *good* and appears to be very *bad*.

In my own line of work, we'd be lost without the word to be honest. Plenty within and outside the criminal justice system love to label this or that person as *evil*, and that seems to cover a multitude of sins. It also gives us a wonderful image of a male with horns on his head, poor orthodontic work, busily rubbing his hands in glee at the next person he can deceive and manipulate to achieve his own terrible ends. *Bad* females can get a separate or sometimes an additional descriptor on top of *evil*, which people of my generation seem to especially like to use to describe a spinster aunt they didn't like growing up, and that is *wicked*. In some senses *wicked* is a word that does even more heavy lifting than *evil*, because now we have in our mind's eye an old, cackling, toothless witch warming her hands at a cauldron as she plans her next despicable act against man or beast.

When it comes to the most serious crimes in criminology, we are firmly wedded to the idea that cold-blooded murderers are typically *evil*. And, by the way, Myra Hindley, infamous for the Moors murders, was evil, and also, of course, wicked. To be fair, you would find very few people who would have difficulty with these two words being applied to either or both of the Moors murderers. And for those of us who love to judge (that would be all of us, by the way), *evil* and *wicked* are the ultimate put downs. There is after all no real comeback after being described by everyone as one or both of those. There's no tablet we can give someone and say to them, "There, there; just take that now and you'll be feeling much less wicked and evil in the morning after a good night's sleep." But it's a great pair of words and they do a great job of judging whoever we may be putting in their box. We do, after all, love to judge people, and, full disclosure here, few would have as much experience as myself in this regard.

It started with a teacher of mine, a Mr. Egan, who I decided (at the tender age of eight no less) wasn't really built for this teaching stuff, and would have been more useful if he had stayed at home on the farm. By the time I had gotten to University College Dublin I thought I was the resurrected James Joyce—which, incidentally, wouldn't have filled Joyce with much confidence. Therefore, other students who did not go around Dublin on a black Nelly bike, with a tweed jacket, a pipe in their mouth, and a copy of Ulysses sticking out of their front basket, I judged to be strange people and nowhere near the sophistication of yours truly.

When I was finished judging the rest of the student population who didn't wear corduroy pants and manage to talk complete gibberish all the time about *Finnegans Wake*, I then, by some quirk of fate, managed to enter the work population. There, I spent the next thirty years judging people who either didn't work in investment banks, didn't lecture in criminology, didn't head up law schools, didn't go to Oxford or Cambridge, and didn't have a lot to say, about everything. In fact, up until recently I took my judging to its natural limits by, well, judging people as a profession when I sat as a magistrate in England. Not only did I and my colleagues judge people, we then had the temerity to pass sentence on them, would you believe.

So when it comes to judging others, that's right, Madam, you are currently looking at Judge Judy. And I hope you won't mind me saying so, but just about all of us engage in this. But I wonder where we humans got this idea that we could pass judgment on others. I mean, the Bible could not be any clearer: judge not and you shall not be judged (Luke 6:37), and treat everyone as you would wish to be treated. As long as you do this to one of the least of my brethren, you do it to me, said Christ (Matt 25:40). Yet we can't seem to stop ourselves, and we just love black-and-white thinking. That person is good; the other person is bad. That person is warm; the other person is wicked. And then, of course, our favorite judging word, unashamedly stolen from God—*evil*. We have even managed to extend the word further into our simplistic idea of our Christian life, which goes something like this.

We live here on earth, then we are either good or bad, and then, depending on this, we go to heaven or hell (with a few theological tweaks along the way that we haven't got time to go into now). *Evil*, we have decided, is, at the very least, used to describe an horrendous human, or, at worst, the devil himself with a flailing tail. And everyone we throw that moniker at is (if they are very lucky) going to hell for all eternity and, one assumes, on a handcart.

Why? Because we said so. Not God, not the Christ we purport to know and love, but us mere mortals. It is we who say that certain others have no more right to live on God's good, clean earth than a weasel. But we have missed a serious trick here, certainly, when it comes to our lives on this planet. Here's a takeaway from today: hell is not somewhere you go after you die. It's here on earth. Evil is not that person over there. It's us. We have created it. Evil therefore is something that we as humans have created when we seized autonomy from God. And that by the way is all of us, not just those we like to say are lesser than us.

C. S. Lewis wisely said in *The Great Divorce* that evil and hell are God's monument to our human dignity and choice.[1] You see, God will honor our decision to reject him but he will not allow this decision of ours to continue to ruin his world. Hell and evil will be *outside* the circle of his city. The new Jerusalem. In the meantime we forget that the only one who can judge is Christ. Or as a friend of mine once succinctly said to me, "John, the only people who should be taking any positions in this life, are Pilates instructors." So when we see Christ engage the word *evil* in the Gospels let's make a decision today that those words are for him and him alone to use and not us. After all, we forfeited that option back in the garden of Eden. What we can do, however, is soak up the actual message of the Gospels, which involves us not judging anyone or giving any person negative descriptions. And so, when Christ said his last earthly goodbyes to his disciples, and therefore by implication the rest of humanity, let us continue to have his words in our hearts and minds. He says, "As you have sent me into the world, so I have sent them into the world. And for their sakes I sanctify myself, so that they also may be sanctified in truth" (John 17:18–19).

---

1. See C. S. Lewis, *The Great Divorce* (New York: HarperOne, 2009), 75.

Part 1: Reflections from the Shadows

Christ says we are sanctified. In other words, we are set apart, we are holy, and not in our own right but because of him. We may be made in his image but, never forget, we are not him and so we cannot judge anyone, except ourselves. So before we decide to use that word *evil* to describe any person in the future, let's all do ourselves a favor. Let's go take a long hard look in the bathroom mirror before we jump to any further conclusions.

The answer might surprise us somewhat.

Every Breath You Take...
The God of Communication

I'M SORRY BUT SOMETIMES when you are looking at Scripture you would be forgiven for asking yourself the question, What in God's name (quite literally) are they all about because at times there appears to be a communications deficit. One Sunday recently, for example, Deuteronomy advised my poor congregation that Israel needed to pay heed to ordinances and statutes (Deut 6:1). Whatever all that means. Somewhat confusingly on the same Sunday, in the Letter from James, God was described as the "Father of lights," which is then followed by something to do with fruits and shadows (Jas 1:17). The Gospel can sometimes appear to enjoy theological gymnastics as it veers between fornication, adultery, and something about defiled hands (Mark 7:1–18). I don't know about you, but it seems to me like it might be time to get the PR gurus in from Saatchi and Saatchi to do some explaining for us. And that's the problem we often cry nowadays.

Leaving aside the word of God, with its seemingly various interpretations, this generation, we say, just doesn't know how to communicate like we did. Well this very conversation came up recently on the breakfast show on BBC Radio 5 in the UK. Some of you may even listen to this station from time to time. Radio 5 Live is a kind of poor man's BBC Radio 4. Plenty of serious stuff all right, but there is always time for yet another sports bulletin to keep the audience's attention.

A listener texted in to say that she could remember when you just needed to dial four digits to get a landline. Now the UK was hugely engaged. Callers from Land's End to John O'Groats were texting in to say that was nothing. They could remember when it was just three digits to get a landline. Matters seemed to stall at that point until a David from Leicester sent in a text for the big reveal. He could remember when you only had to

Part 1: Reflections from the Shadows

dial two digits to get a landline number. Britain was silent. Surely no one could beat that. Or could they? Well they hadn't allowed for John in Dublin (that would be me, by the way) who thought it was time to put those English to the sword. I carefully penned my text which went exactly as follows to the presenters:

> Hi, Rachel and Rick. As a kid in the 1970s my aunt lived in Ballycastle in Mayo in Ireland. In those days you simply rang zero and asked for one digit, namely Ballycastle eight, and, hey presto, there was my Mayo auntie at the other end of the phone. Somewhat comically she would always answer the phone, "Eight Speaking." Even more comically the operator in the village once interrupted our conversation and asked me not to be too cheeky to her.

Well you can only imagine that when they read this out, the two presenters were sent into great mirth and congratulations. "Dublin John," as I was now known, had won the day they said, and no one, least of all an Englishman, could beat a one-digit number.

You see, back in the day we knew how to communicate, we tell ourselves. It was all nice and simple, and maybe even only one digit *would* do it. In fact, communication was so boundaried in those days, a call in the evening on the landline could send the household into a state of shock. For example, I distinctly remember our house receiving a call one Sunday evening around 10:00 p.m. in the early 1970s. My mother got so worried about this, she called our local police station to advise them of this horrific event. She was then (genuinely) advised by the sergeant on duty that she wasn't to worry about it now, but that if we got another call to give them a shout. Mind you, presumably at that point it would be too late for the police to call them back, so the mystery caller would have had to wait until the morning. Today, of course, the younger generation, and let's be honest here, the *not* so younger generation, have no issues allegedly communicating all the time. We have taken this communication thing to levels that previous generations could only have ever dreamed of. I mean, we have the evidence of this, isn't that right? We are on our devices morning, noon, and night, so we must be communicating at a whole new level.

Wait. Houston, we have a problem. The truth is that we are the generation who live beside, on, and sometimes in our smart devices. We feel the need to comment and share *everything* we experience in life from our latest main course in a restaurant in a one-horse town to us lying on a beach drinking a Babycham (that's one for the older readers, by the way). The

Every Breath You Take . . .

truth is that in a time when we have never shared *so* much, never has there been a generation who managed to listen so *little*. We fire mindless buckets of entirely useless and narcissistic information out to any other device that may receive it. Then we fret when comments fail to praise us for the latest picture of someone's homemade soup in their garden shed, or, worse still, they are negative. You see, we're sometimes better off when we say nothing at all. Less is always more, but somewhere, somehow, someone managed to steal this script. And then there is God. I mean, he doesn't even use social media (totes awks . . .), at least not that we are aware of. How can we possibly communicate with him? More importantly, how can he communicate with us, because, you see, we are very busy putting up mindless posts on Facebook. So if he wants our attention, well, he's going to have the join the social media queue, isn't that right?

We are busy, and, by the way, that is B. U. S. Y. in social media script. And, really, Scripture, like I mentioned earlier, doesn't help because frankly it contains language and ideas from another time. "Cutesy" at best perhaps, as the young people might say, but not really relevant. Yet if we just put our mobile phones down for one minute, close the lid of our laptops, or put our iPads to bed for an afternoon nap we might begin to see things more clearly. Like we perhaps used to.

God has and will continue to be the King of communication. It is we who don't return his calls. Remember, he is before you now in the person you may be sitting beside or near. He is with them in *their* joy and in *their* suffering, just like he is in *yours*. He was in those seats where you sit sometimes on a Sunday, with hundreds, maybe thousands of churchgoers from times past who prayed just like you. Maybe they were even better at it. He communicates to us in our waking, and our going down, and during all the bits in between. He was with us and held our hand when we came from our mothers' wombs, and it will be he who will hold it one last time when we set off on our final journey. And remember, he is and has always been, in our *every* breath.

In Hebrew, his name is spelled *YHWH*. But how we do we pronounce that? It's impossible, right? It has no vowels. But then we look very closely and we see that this name is actually in the sound of every breath we have taken since the day we were born. Try it now by noticing your breath in and your breath out. Listen to the sound.

YAH—WAY
YAH—WAY
YAH—WAY

Part 1: Reflections from the Shadows

And that is how God communicates with us: through every breath we take. So now, and while we still have enough breath left in our bodies, it's time for us to return his call.

Sabbath Secrets
Hiding in Full View

You know, the word *Sabbath* isn't a word we hear very often anymore. The word comes from the Hebrew word *Shabbat*, which means "to cease" or "to rest." And it of course reflects the biblical creation narrative in Genesis where God created the world in six days and rested on the seventh day. I say "of course" but if you were to actually use the word today to young people, they would look at you aghast and have you sectioned. After all, "Karen, I'll meet you at McDonald's at noon on the Sabbath" is not a normal cry from the younger generation today. Or any generation, come to think of it. The Sabbath is meant to be a time for rest, worship, and reflection on spiritual and ethical values. Its observance has evolved over time but continues to allegedly be a central element of religious life for some of us, one day a week, with the big Sabbath heads on us.

Now I know what you are thinking. John, you are saying, sure, no one really observes Sabbath anymore in terms of their belief. And for the few that do even they are straight off down to Tesco afterward, mowing the lawn, watching the football, fighting with the wife (in fact, occasionally doing all three at the same time), and generally being about as nonobservant of this rest and reflection day as is humanly possible. I see others of you now thinking back to the old days of Sabbath. The days when not only did we dress up for Sunday worship but there were even lads working in the fields who had a tie and shirt on with the standard V-necked jumper and the baggy pants. The day was observed as one of rest and religious devotion. Many people refrained from unnecessary work, in line with both the Roman Catholic Church and Christian churches more generally. As well as Sunday service, activities might include prayer, Sunday school, reading the Bible, or participating in parish events.

Part 1: Reflections from the Shadows

Most shops and businesses were closed on Sundays. The concept of a *day of rest* extended to the commercial sector meaning that the streets were quieter and economic activity was minimal. In Ireland, for example, pubs had restricted hours on Sundays, often opening only in the evening. Many in that country, may remember that pubs were only allowed to open for a short period in the afternoon, typically from 12:30 to 2:00 p.m. This brief window, which we comically referred to as the "holy hour," was intended to allow patrons to have a drink after attending church. God love us, we must have been exceptionally thirsty from all that praying. After closing in the early afternoon, pubs would reopen in the evening from 7:00 to 10:00 p.m. These evening hours allowed for socializing later in the day, but still maintained a relatively early closing time compared to the rest of the week. Indeed, if you wanted a drink after 2:00 p.m. you had better have a strong pair of legs on you, because you would have to peddle very hard to get to what were known as the "bona fides" outside Dublin with their more liberal opening hours. In this regard, there was a strong rumor that my own father had the most well-developed cycling legs in Dublin.

You see, Christ is in no doubt about the Sabbath, in Mark for example, when he says to his disciples, "the Sabbath was made for man, not man for the Sabbath" (Mark 2:27). So though it appears that we may have to a large extent forgotten the Sabbath, it would appear the Sabbath has not forgotten us. And yet still in our minds we hark back to the old days of our Sundays, and we feel those days are gone and that we may somehow have lost a little bit of ourselves in the transition. Many of us after all were the generations that walked not just to church on a Sunday and back, but to school and back, and, in fact, to everywhere else and back. We were the generations that did our homework alone to get out as soon as possible to play in the street, that collected sports cards, that found, collected, washed, and returned empty coke bottles to the local shop for a halfpenny or a dime each and then, if we were lucky, bought a sherbet Dip Dab, a packet of Kola Cubes, and a bottle of fizzy cola.

We were the generation whose rented TVs ended at 11:00 p.m. once the announcer bid us good evening, and on went the National Anthem. For many of us, we were the generation that had parents who were there, and, yes, whose Sundays never, ever changed. But for better or for worse, everything has changed and we had better get used to it, not least how we negotiate our Sundays today. But perhaps, just perhaps, we have been looking at this Sabbath thing in the wrong way all along. Recently, while working as a prison chaplain, I was talking to a life prisoner and he asked me what I was doing for the weekend. I said, Just going to see a football match with my son. When I asked him about his own weekend, he said, "I'm 'just relaxing' John." "I love Saturdays especially," he said. "The pressure is off." Quite why pressure is less on a Saturday compared to any other day of the week for your average inmate is anyone's guess, but for prisoner No. D4510 this was his Sabbath.

In fact, that evening I did go to see my little football team play another little football team, and we actually scored a goal, and then the music came blaring over the dodgy Tannoy. And, as ever, it was The Cure's famous hit "It's Friday I'm in Love," of which the opening lyrics say it all. You really should go look them up right now; I'll wait.

You see, in one very real sense, there is no one day when we should open up God to a visit. It's every day. Sure, we can keep aside a special day for him and, as Christ tells us, the Sabbath may not be a bad start. But if the Lord is truly "Lord of the Sabbath" as we have heard in Mark, then the Sabbath cannot be just one day of the week. The Sabbath is every waking moment of our lives—every second when we are asked to live in God's love and, most importantly, show that love to all those around us at all times, and most especially when we believe they least deserve it. Perhaps in this regard we should leave the last words to that prisoner No. D4510. I asked sometime back what he was most looking forward to about the coming week. His answer? "My cellmate isn't being released after all. He has more charges coming down the track. It will be nice to still have him as company."

You see, sometimes the true meaning of the Sabbath can be about much more than we ever knew and far simpler than we ever thought: *love*.

When the End Is the Beginning
Life Ages, Death Restores

Now some of you may have noticed in recent times something that might have taken you by surprise. It came from research conducted on Generation Z, or, as they are sometimes known, the "zoomers." Now just to remind you, Gen Z are those who are born between the mid-1990s and early 2000s, so they are roughly between fifteen and thirty years of age. (Incidentally, in case you were wondering, their parents are Generation X or older millennials, and they were born between 1965 and the early 1980s, so are about forty to fifty-nine years of age.)

But back to those Gen Z persons between fifteen and thirty years of age. We now officially have an age when you cross into the word *old* according to this group. Whatever you thought it might be, put it on hold. But before I tell you what this group regard as old, think back to your own childhood and what you thought qualified as old in those days. I know I can remember a six-year-old yours truly going into first class and looking at my teacher, a Mr. Egan, and thinking what an astonishingly elderly person he was to be teaching us. How was he still alive, I asked myself, let alone able to stand up unaided? His speech seemed incoherent, he had wrinkles, and was that a bald patch I noticed? To add insult to aging injury, he shuffled around like a nonagenarian waiting for their pension in a post office queue. I was to discover before I left the school that he could in fact have been no more than twenty-eight at the time, but to a six-year-old he was my image of Methuselah.

As life went on, I never really changed and basically worked on the premise, (like a lot of you still do, I'm guessing), that anyone older than me, was old. As a twenty-year-old university student, I remember hearing the news that someone I knew was having a twenty-fifth birthday party and

When the End Is the Beginning

thinking how brave of them it was to make a public statement about how very, very old they were. In fact, I can even recall my mother coming back from our local bank branch delighted that she would now be able to reap all the benefits of what they called in those days the "golden oldie account." She had reached fifty at the time and I thought that her bank was being very kind indeed calling *only* a fifty-year-old person old. How were those ancient thirty-somethings getting away with it I said to myself.

But now the Gen Z types are telling us what age they regard as crossing into old, and that, ladies and gentlemen, is apparently fifty-seven. That's it. Once you have hit the high end of your mid-fifties, it's "Say goodnight to the folks, Gracie." Of course it would be interesting to talk to the Gen Zers when they are fifty-seven themselves and they might take a view more like us then. In other words, there is one simple rule as mentioned: the truth is you still qualify as old if you are older than I. Yet regardless of the age we view as old, or how the number gets pushed out each generation as medicine improves, one fact we all know, even if we have not yet fully appreciated it, is that all our time is limited in this life. And we know this especially because we have close relations and dear friends who have died at varying ages.

A grandparent, a mother or father, an aunt or uncle, a brother or sister, wife or husband, or maybe even especially, tragically, a son or daughter. Regardless, age gets thrown at us a lot when someone we love dies. That ninety-year-old mother "had a good innings," we say, and "she's better off where she is," we proudly announce. I wonder did many of us think to ask the view of this relatively healthy ninety-year-old mother before we made these statements? But we can make some sense in our heads of the older person dying. They lived some sort of life and, hopefully, loved and were loved. But a young person? No. That makes no sense to us at all. Ever. I know some of you reading this will have lost your own children, so you people know only too well what I am talking about.

After all, what if your son was a beautiful twenty-year-old boy who tragically and violently lost his life in the blink of an eye while simply answering a door to a stranger in the middle of the day? What would that feel like for those he left behind? Jimmy was one such boy, and the son of friends of mine, and on February 24, 2018, he inexplicably went to meet our God in the blink of an eye, his life cruelly ended by a psychiatrically disturbed man. A man, incidentally, whom he had never met. What can we ever say, as a community and church, to Jimmy's family to give them comfort in their darkest hour?

Not a great deal, for God surely lies best in the silence. However, what we can do is to point them and ourselves to Scripture and take our pick. You see, God's response to such times is written up in bold letters for us all to see. For example, John says that the gift of the Holy Spirit, the gift of love, was poured out, even on the gentiles, and we know that "Everyone who believes that Jesus is the Christ has been born of God, and everyone who loves the parent, loves the child" (1 John 5:1). Both most of all and herein lies the true key to Christ's love for us and why we never die: when we hear from Christ that "This is my commandment, that you love one another as I have loved you. No one has greater love than this, to lay down one's life for one's friends" (John 15:12–13).

Parents who have children do that all the time for their kids; they love them and there may no comparable love to this, for that is all we ever have to do as parents, as sons and daughters, as husbands and wives, as brothers and sisters. It is simply to love. When you are looking for Christ in the darkest abyss of your life, remember John tells us in another famous passage, "Anyone who does not love, does not know God, because God *is* love" (1 John 4:8; emphasis added). So when you grieve for those you love, that is Christ beside and with you. And it is a love that never leaves us, for all of this life, or the next. It is the love that Jimmy's parents and sisters and countless like them have for those they loved but who have gone to Christ before them. So these beautiful parts of our lives are never gone. They are always with us; they are here with us right now as you read this reflection. The truth is they are with us at our rising and our going down.

But I would like to leave my final words if I may with Jimmy, and all those sons and daughters, beloved relations, and dear friends, who have gone before us. These words by poet Elizabeth Frye have been written into many obituary cards and you may have heard them said before. But now we really listen, and then at last we truly know that all the people we loved like Jimmy will always be with us.

> Do not stand at my grave and weep
> I am not there. I do not sleep.
> I am a thousand winds that blow.
> I am the diamond glints on snow.
> I am the sunlight on ripened grain.
> I am the gentle autumn rain.
> When you awaken in the morning's hush

When the End Is the Beginning

I am the swift uplifting rush
Of quiet birds in circled flight.
I am the soft stars that shine at night.
Do not stand at my grave and cry;
I am not there. I did not die.[1]

---

1. Mary Elizabeth Frye, "Do Not Stand at My Grave and Weep," PoemHunter.com, Feb. 2, 2015, www.poemhunter.com/poem/do-not-stand-at-my-grave-and-weep.

Mind the Dash
Careful of That Bit Between Birth and Death

As Christians, at various times of the year we start to think about birth and, indeed, death. After all, the birth of Jesus Christ is not a trivial affair, nor indeed his death. Come to think of it and truth be told, we are also perhaps a little worried about our own passing. Until, of course, we get distracted with TV, social media, kids, grandkids, and just about anything that will keep us away from this topic. Death is all very well, but in our experience to date that is something which happens everyone else.

Now, I don't need to tell you about how we like to celebrate Jesus' birth around Christmas. If a Martian were to come down during the festive season to see how we were getting on, they would be amazed about the devotion there appears to be to the birth of Jesus Christ around the world. "Baby Jesus" this, "Kings of Orient" that, and "manger" the other. What a faithful bunch we all are. Hmm. A little closer inspection reveals, of course, that this devotion may be more about alcohol, food, and gifts, and rather less about the adoration of the Savior by the magi. The same Martian might get an even bigger surprise around Easter time. What appears to be an unrivaled devotion to the death and resurrection of Jesus Christ seems to be equally about shoving as many creme eggs into one's face as if chocolate egg prohibition was about to be brought in. Regardless, we do love to mark a birth, and a death, and we make a big deal about those two events. A really big deal. My late mother just loved a good funeral, and when I asked her why, she responded because she was still alive to see them. Fair.

Yet something strange happens when we visit graves, as many of us may sadly do over a year. Note, there are only two dates that are of any relevance on each tombstone and are up in stark, bold letters. The year of a person's birth, and the year of their death. That is all that matters it would

Mind the Dash

appear: the beginning and the end. These are the bookends to our existence in this finite place. That's it. Two simple dates sum up our entire earthly existence. But wait. There is something we are missing. There is a small but crucial part to that line that we always miss. In fact, there is a poem that has been doing the rounds on social media in recent times by a woman called Linda Ellis which attempts to clarify the matter. She is bravely suggesting that we start to think very differently about these two dates.

In fact, she is asking us to take our focus completely away from these two years and instead focus on the small, forgotten bit in the middle that joins them up: the dash.

I wonder, if we were all to be really honest with ourselves, how is our dash going? You see, while we are all obsessing about births and deaths, how are we all *really* getting on with the bit in the middle? The bit that we call *life*. For example, Isaiah talks about his people greatly rejoicing in the LORD and exulting in their God because of all he has done. Indeed, he goes further. Apparently for Zion's sake we will not keep silent, and for Jerusalem's sake we will not rest, until her vindication shines out like the dawn, and her salvation like a burning torch (Isa 62:1).

But is that truly how we might sum up our Christmases and Easters past and present? Was it *really* all about glorifying Christ and doing what he has asked of us, or were we more guilty of our usual "seasonal showtime" for ourselves and others? Drink, food, chocolate, and making merry, and lots of it. If you like, excess in all areas. There is nothing wrong with that of course as long as it is very much a bit player in our seasonal worship. Luke, after all, arguably gives us some permission to be excited about the birth of Christ and surely celebrate his arrival when he says, "The shepherds returned, glorifying and praising God for all they had heard and seen, as it had been told them" (Luke 2:20).

But what about the bit in the middle? The bit that is our lives on this earth? How is that dash working for us do we think? With the permission of Isaiah and Luke, I encourage you to look up the words of "The Dash" by Linda Ellis and read this extraordinary poem for yourself.

Thank you Linda. Now if you will excuse me, I have to . . . uhm . . . dash.

Jaw-Dropping

Time to Discover the Outer and Inner Cosmos

Now I'm going to start us all off on a depressing note. It is after all raining outside (other climates are available). It would be rude of me not to. And this downbeat note comes from the famous philosopher Bertrand Russell courtesy of his 1903 essay "A Free Man's Worship" when he said the following: "All the labor of all the ages, all the devotion, all the inspiration, all the noonday brightness of human genius are destined to extinction."[1] So now, my friends, if that is true, what is the point?

Oh dear. So I need something to make me feel better. Something that says to me that, John, you are not just an incomprehensible, if hugely attractive, speck in the universe who came from nothing and will return to nothing. So I turn to the book of Genesis as I always do in such times. It, after all, calms me down and gives me meaning. You see, Genesis does exactly what it says on the tin. As we know, it seemingly neatly describes the earth's beginnings. Listen to these simple but effective words again: "In the beginning when God created the heavens and the earth, the earth was a formless void and darkness covered the face of the deep, while a wind from God swept over the face of the waters. Then God said, 'Let there be light'; and there was light" (Gen 1:1–3).

Fantastic, we have said for in or around two millennia. That's that, then so. There was nothing, and then there was something, and a chap called God sorted all that out. We were delighted with ourselves. We didn't need to give all that universe thing too much thought, and to be frank it's too big anyway for us to be thinking about because right now we've got to do the shopping, and, sure, hubby will soon be looking for his dinner. After

---

1. Bertrand Russell, *Why I Am Not a Christian: And Other Essays on Religion and Related Subjects*, ed. Paul Edwards (New York: Simon and Schuster, 1957), 107–8.

Jaw-Dropping

all, thinking about the eternal void in space is all very well but it won't do the washing. But not to worry, we have Genesis and it sorted everything out anyway. Then suddenly, maybe it didn't. It started with Einstein's theory of relativity and, frankly, for the strict seven-day creationists, things have been looking a little wobbly ever since.

The problem appears to be with those nasty old astrophysicists and cosmologists of the last couple of centuries from Einstein to Carl Sagan right up to Stephen Hawking and Brian Greene. These lads appear to be messing with our delicate little religious heads. You see, we now know for a scientific fact, and thanks to what is known as cosmic microwave background radiation (which I promise not to go into), that our universe is actually 13.7 billion years old, give or take a million years here or there. You know, they say church congregations are getting older, but 13.7 billion years old? Now that's a really long time to be shuffling around.

But wait. Everything could be far, far older than that. Our big bang, we are being told by some, could in fact have been preceded by millions of other big bangs, a concept known as the inflationary universe.[2] The galaxy that we call the Milky Way might seem big yet relatively self-contained to our small minds, but it has about maybe 200 billion stars itself. And remember, it's only one galaxy. There are estimated to be at least 170 billion galaxies and, wait for this, maybe as many as two trillion, or even between six and twenty trillion, plus exponentially more stars in the universe.[3] I hope you're all still with me. As a result of which many cosmologists extrapolate from this and suggest there may in fact have been no beginning to time, and the universe may have *always* been here. So wrap your heads around that one today.

So the question is, Where we do we believers go with all of this? How do we reconcile faith and physics? Well there is good argument to say that theology and belief are nothing without physics, and, indeed, it is very persuasive to argue that physics is a wonderful explanation of God's laws. The intelligent design and fine tuning arguments of the universe, as to the existence of a prime mover, are, without a doubt, persuasive. There's even something to the counterarguments based on the multiverse, in other

---

2. Ethan Siegel, "The Strongest Evidence for a Universe Before the Big Bang," Starts with a Bang, *Big Think*, Mar. 16, 2023, https://bigthink.com/starts-with-a-bang/evidence-universe-before-big-bang.

3. Ethan Siegel, "Our Universe Has More Galaxies Than Carl Sagan Ever Imagined," Starts with a Bang, *Big Think*, Dec. 25, 2024, https://bigthink.com/starts-with-a-bang/galaxies-in-universe.

words, that there are infinite numbers of universes beyond ours and so naturally, in one corner, of one speck, of one little universe, the ingredients that allow life to exist are sure to be in place. And by the way, even if the multiverse argument turns out to be correct, it should not have one jot of influence on our faith in God. If anything, it may increase it. Let me tell you why. The next time you meet a faith speed bump and you hear someone else deriding the book of Genesis or the Bible generally because they don't understand what metaphor is, then as that 1970s popular UK band Showaddywaddy said, take three steps to heaven.

Step one: Look around you. Look at this earth in all its beauty and design. We sometimes call this natural theology. Read more about the cosmos and the theories that surround its beginning, and possible demise. Come back to me then and lets have a discussion about what scientific evidence you will have that nothing can come from nothing, and how *nothing* (i.e., *nonbeing*) can easily spontaneously create itself into trillions of universes and life-forms. As some Minister I once knew would have said, "Good luck with that." Step two: What about jumping into the divine word, the Bible, and reading around it? Trust me, once you begin to unravel that book in even the smallest way, it's a game changer. Step three: Look at your family, your friends, and the beauty of life that surrounds you. Look how you care (or sometimes don't care) for others. Think about your conscience, your mind, the very fact that you can build, create, and design in the most remarkable ways. Most of all, think about how you love, and, if you are lucky enough, are loved. Consider any one or all of these three steps the next time you are having a faith speed wobble, and God will surely reappear before you.

Do not, however, do this as some psychological trick to play on yourself so as you don't get too panicky. Rather, because of the sheer weight of evidence that surrounds you of God's existence in your every waking moment. Evidence that shows you that you are loved and treasured more than you can ever imagine by the one who came before us and whose sandals we are not worthy to untie.

"Be not afraid," Christ tells us, "I go before you always, come follow me, and I will give you rest." If we remember nothing else, we remember that.

Can't Get No Satisfaction?
God Can Help

SOME OF YOU MAY have noticed in recent years that Mick Jagger celebrated his eightieth birthday. All the greats (and not so greats) were there: Ronnie Wood, Jerry Hall, Angelica Huston, Lenny Kravitz, Stella McCartney, and, of course, what party would be complete without Leonardo DiCaprio. There's one for the ladies. And that's without me even mentioning the exotic Cuban dancers.

Apparently it was a "wild" party, which certainly says something about the other octogenarians who must have wondered if they would ever be getting back to bed because of this "Jumpin' Jack Flash" (see what I did there?). The media subsequently reported Sir Michael Philip Jagger, how shall we say, being "led out" at 4:00 a.m. by another gentleman who looked as if could do with having been "led out" himself. So you might reasonably ask the question, What exactly is *wrong* (or right) with Mick Jagger? What makes an octogenarian who looks like he could do with a good iron and a haircut, gyrate on a dance floor until the middle of a night in an emerald-green suit that gives the impression of a confused leprechaun?

Well, you might answer, an awful lot of money and an awful lot of fame. But, you know, I think the answer goes deeper than that, and oddly enough Mick Jagger himself had the very answer to that question, nearly sixty years ago. You see Mick Jagger couldn't get no satisfaction then, and it would appear he's still having difficulty getting it now.

Well I'm sure generations are grateful to Mr. Jagger for his profound words over the years, and, while it's probably fair to say they are unlikely to win any poetry prize, there's probably more in his words and lifestyle that mirror our own than we might care to admit—without the flashier bits, of course. The truth is that, like the Rolling Stones, none of us are ever satisfied. As Mick would say, we simply can't get none.

You see, during our lives we have wanted the best that this world could offer us for ourselves and, subsequently, our families. We thought it would be critical to get the best education and/or employment and diligently go into the office and work very, very hard indeed, or our own world would fall apart. Of course it would not, and it did not. We are still here. Then we all continue this charade in our middle lives. Private school fees, big holidays, nice cars, and constantly taking about, if not actually, upgrading our homes. That's to say nothing of the little bolt-hole in Spain, France, or the Hamptons. Not to mention the obsessive harvesting of money more generally to create a pension pot that would support a small state.

Many of us passed the point of comfortable and necessary living a long time ago, and yet still we can't get no satisfaction. And look at us now reading this today, and me writing away, all thinking to ourselves, well there may be some truth in all of that, but things are different as I get older and *now* I have focus on what is really important. Plot twist! No; we don't. We still think about money, nice cars, holidays, lunches; and even if we are no longer thinking about them as much for ourselves (because we have more than enough) we now think about all these things for our children and grandchildren.

So the question is really not, What is wrong with Mick Jagger? but, What is wrong with us? Isaiah often goes to the heart of this very question. He tells us to come, buy wine and milk but this time without money and without price. For why do we spend money on that which is not bread, and our labor for that which does not satisfy us (Isa 55:1–2)? You see, when all the Mercedes, Lexus, (other luxury makes are available) and perks are set aside, and when we finally slump in our chairs with our lives strewn beside us on the cutting room floor of life, where will we say we got our satisfaction as we come before the Christ we purport to know and love? This world offers us many, many temporary and empty pursuits, and trust me when I say that there are few people who probably know this better than I do. God is hiding in full view and yet still we cannot see him properly. He is waiting for us to satisfy our souls, not our bellies or our cultural narcissism. And all we have to do, which we hear in Isaiah and across Scripture, is to listen carefully to him, and eat what is good.

We must simply incline our ears and come to him so that we may live, and then he will make with us an everlasting covenant, which is his

Can't Get No Satisfaction?

love for us (Isa 55:3). From the day we are born our time is limited, so let's remember that our road to hell is paved with all our good intentions. Let us therefore truly listen to Isaiah and take the right turn on the road to Christ. So the next time you can't get no satisfaction in your life, well, you can't say that you didn't know where to look.

Now, if you will excuse me, I have some moves to practice with my walking frame.

You'll Never Walk Alone
If You Keep Christ in Your Heart

Jürgen Klopp. There. I've said it. And I know what you're thinking. There are not many polemics across the globe that will typically begin with that name. And I'll come back to Jürgen, former manager of Liverpool FC. But for those who are too posh to even think of football, let alone consider the manager of one team, let me assist with this first. It's not immediately easy to explain why grown men can find themselves so intrinsically linked to any football club, let alone one across the water in another country, but guess what? I'm going to give it a go. When I was growing up on the mean streets of Dublin, my father was obsessed with Liverpool FC. Now, he had as much connection to Liverpool as I have to men's synchronized swimming. That's right, Madam. Very little.

Yet once BBC's *Match of the Day* theme tune began on a Saturday night with a smiling Jimmy Hill beaming down on us, or, indeed, Brian Moore in *The Big Match* on a Sunday, my dad was so full of shock and awe, I thought on occasion he might pass out. Once Liverpool appeared, however, with maybe Emlyn Hughes or Stevie Heighway or a host of other characters of the day performing their footballing magic, it was as if Scotty himself from the starship *Enterprise* had beamed him up. And that started to rub off on me. Suddenly I found myself hyperventilating when Liverpool played. It became very important that they didn't lose, and when they did there was extraordinary wailing and gnashing of teeth. Mainly my own.

A few years back my son and I went to Anfield in Liverpool for a match, as we do, and decided to take the stadium tour. When I touched that "This is Anfield" sign as you come out of the players' tunnel, I can share with you now that I genuinely had an out-of-body experience. When Liverpool play these days my son and I have a routine as to where we sit, when we take our breaks from the match—and how we take them, and the avoidance at all costs of any predictions, good, bad, or indifferent. We are quite the dad-son couple but our psychiatrist says we are coming on in leaps and bounds. But then Jürgen Klopp, Liverpool's most iconic manager of recent years, said he was leaving *us*.

Jürgen Norbert Klopp, after a relatively indifferent enough footballing career at a German club, Mainz, where he was for most of his playing life, then went into management, and the rest, as they say, is the stuff of history. This was, however, surely the end of an era. The one certainty we had at Liverpool FC was Jürgen Klopp. How could he ever abandon us? He was, after all, our anchor. Our ballast in every storm. Bill Shankly, Bob Paisley, Kenny Dalgish? We are only *just* getting over them leaving, and now this? Truth be told, it's not really about the football, whatever team you might support in any arena. That's just a news peg for us to show out best characteristics as human beings. Family, togetherness, a tribe, security, and, most importantly, so much love, howsoever we may direct it.

Yet sadly, as we all know, nothing lasts forever, at least not on this earth. Stars are born and die, we lose jobs, the kids grow up, a few grandkids may appear for some of us if we are lucky, and then, yes, we shuffle off only for another generation to imagine that they have been the ones to discover everything about everything. As everyone before them has also thought.

And yes, it appears that even Jürgen Klopp has a sell-by date. No one ever said this living thing was easy. So the times may be always a-changin', but as Jesus says in Scripture, "No one puts new wine into old wineskins; otherwise, the wine will burst the skins, and the wine is lost, and so are the skins; but one puts new wine into fresh wineskins" (Mark 2:22). In other words, the old and the new don't mix. Holidays will end, jobs will come and go, people will fall out and make up, and, yes, even football managers will fade into the mist of time, but life moves on. What we thought was so, so important last week, will have zero relevance today, and, trust me, as we are about to go home to God, the only thing that will count was if we loved as best we could and, if we are lucky, were also loved, in God's name.

So amid all the scary changes we may have in our life, we have one, sure constant. He is the God who was there with my dad when he cried tears of sadness when Liverpool lost the FA Cup in 1972 to Arsenal and again, tears of joy, when they won in 1974 against Newcastle. Just like Christ has been with me and my son any time we have gone to Anfield in recent years and I've held back the tears when, before each game, the stadium sings, "You'll

Part 1: Reflections from the Shadows

Never Walk Alone." But he is with us all, and at all times, and through all our trials and tribulations. And I will let you in on a little secret: he is with us here right now as you read this.

Think of that for one moment. Right now. So when all the football games are over, all the parties ended, the careers come to a close, and your GP starts to look more like your best friend than your doctor, such is the frequency of your visits, know one thing. As Ps 139 says the Lord knit us together in our mothers' wombs, and before he formed us, he knew us. Everything passes and becomes renewed as we learn from Mark's Gospel. And, most importantly, that includes us, when on the last day we will be with God as we dwell in the new heavens and the new earth. We, the pieces of unshrunk cloth, will then be beautifully woven in the new cloth—the cloth, that is our Lord and Savior (Matt 9:16).

So we remember, once we are with Christ, when we walk through that storm, we hold our head up high, and never again will we be afraid of the dark.

Judging Others
For a Living

For the last number years, each month or so, I have been going over to Newcastle and Sunderland, in the UK, for a few days, where I sit as a magistrate. We have the same powers as a district judge there, so can sentence for up to two years on more than one count and the vast majority, about 95 percent of cases, are dealt with in those same magistrate courts. Now you won't be surprised to hear from me that you see some shocking sights standing before you, regardless of the alleged crime. I can advise you of two men who, on separate occasions, came in to court wheezing and coughing, sitting in wheelchairs, only for both of them, once they were found not guilty, to jump up Lazarus-like and start walking out of the court. Actually, in one case, he ran out of the court. One woman in her seventies (I repeat, seventies) gave a type of Gettysburg address at the beginning of her trial on the horrors of drugs and drug pushers only to be then found guilty herself of storing, possessing, and supplying heroin, cocaine, and assorted other Class A drugs.

Judges, especially those at street level, just love to, well . . . judge. You might even say to me, "Well, John, isn't that what they (and you) are meant to do?" Well, yes, but of course it should be not a random judgment. Rather it must be one based on all the information we have before us, sprinkled as ever, we hope, with human compassion for both the offender and the offended. And of course the reason any person is found guilty or not guilty in court is because of one word, *evidence*, and its strength—or otherwise. Now magistrates love retiring to consider their verdict and, most of all, to mull over the evidence. The reality may be somewhat different, however. Contrary to popular belief among the criminal fraternity, many magistrates may even be human, and so some of them have made up their mind by one look at the defendant, long before the evidence was ever presented.

Perhaps even more surprisingly, a few others think that no one is ever *really* guilty of any crime, ever, even if the defendant says, "It was me what dun it your worships and you lot have got me banged to rights" (or words to that effect). Magistrates are a very mixed assortment, and you have to trust me on that one. In case you're wondering about yours truly and my ability to deliver fair justice, one presiding magistrate I sat with one day described me as being like a bag of sherbets and Kola Cubes, all rolled into one. When I asked him what he meant he said, "Somewhat spicy but with an ability to deliver sweetly." Thanks. I think . . .

Yet we can't get away from it. Evidence remains very important to the human condition—and when it comes to our faith, well frankly, we just can't get enough of it. The fact that we are told by Jesus that those of us who have *not* seen and yet believe will be blessed still seems more of a message for those few A+ students of belief who've pulled away from the rest of the class. For the rest of us, hovering around more pedestrian grade point averages, our human condition remains that we crave muscular certainties in which to embed our faith. Truth is, we understand the biblical doubting Thomas of John 20:24–29. John's Gospel is full of doubt and cries for evidence. The Jews, for example, did not believe the blind man was even blind in the first place (John 9:18). After all, the alleged miracle needed more robust evidence. Time and time again the man tries to tell them but still they can't, or won't, understand. I mean even his parents are saying, don't be asking us. "I have told you already, and you would not listen," the man says. "Why do you want to hear it again?" (9:27). Exasperated, he says, "Never since the world began has it been heard that anyone opened the eyes of a person born blind" (9:32). Yet their skepticism is okay, as is ours. Doubts and hesitancy are, after all, evidence (pun intended) of the human condition. You see, we just love proof in our everyday lives, yet our faith cynicism is all the more curious when you think about it really.

For example, it remains contested as to what came before the big bang, how long a proton lives, or, indeed, whether the universe is infinite or (in the manner of Father Dougal, in that Channel 4 sitcom of sitcoms, *Father Ted*) just something very, very big. Yet still we never doubt science's ability to get us to foundational truths. Christ seems not to get as much slack. No matter how many times he evidences himself and his truth to us in the Bible, such as when he makes the blind man see, we remain skeptical. We may not necessarily need irrefutable proof, but we do want evidence. We are the "beyond reasonable doubt" generation and Christ needs to sort this out, and not in the moment but in the instant, for we are the "want it all/have it all" kids and we can stop for no man, or God.

Jesus certainly wants us to see the evidence of the Lord's greatness and love for us, but he also wants us to look in the *right* place for it. As Christ said himself, "I came into this world for judgement so that those who do not see may see, and those who do see, may become blind" (John 9:39). Aside from Scripture, the clearest *evidence* for Jesus remains in our going down in the evening and our waking in the morning. It is present in the compassion and the resilience we can show toward our families, and for each other. It is in the everyday wonder of creation and nature. The evidence for Jesus is love.

And the best news of all? This evidence is right around in front of us here and always will be.

Suffer Little Children
One Boy's Suffering . . .

As a young adolescent boy, I had a number of obsessions, one of which included tartan linen pants. I know, go figure. Soon, however, another one was to come into view. The much maligned discotheque, ladies and gentlemen. But before you come to any conclusions, not for me, the terrors of a disco in North Dublin called Tamangos, even if it was "where the gang goes." (How we laughed at that one). No, for my young and remarkably disjointed head there was only one place to be on a Friday night and that was a place called Old Wesley, because that was where every uncomplicated child from South County Dublin went—and, needless to say, I fitted that description perfectly. Indeed, such was my hope for the evening, preparations would begin on Thursday night. "Mother, did you get the dry shampoo?" I would shout. "What do you want with dry shampoo, John?" she would reply. "You don't have enough hair." Now leaving aside the fact that a mother shouldn't be alerting a thirteen-year-old boy to early-onset male-pattern baldness, I forgave her that once she gave me her dry shampoo.

Remember, for those of us in Britain and Ireland this was the era of Mud, Slade, Wizard, Marc Bolan, and the Bay City Rollers no less, and I was going to be up there with the best of them with my wavy, if somewhat numerically challenged, locks. One Friday I particularly remember, school could not end soon enough. Myself and the other boys were meeting up on the cool, hip, if highly residential streets near the event, and we were going to walk down to Old Wesley. Once there, we would presumably rip up some moves on the dance floor for the assembled young ladies. I mean, after all, what could be more impressive than a thirteen-year-old boy in platform shoes, a cheesecloth shirt, and astonishingly flared corduroy pants? (That's right. I had moved on from the linen trousers).

Suffer Little Children

When mother decided, however, at 5:00 p.m. one particular evening that I couldn't go because my Aunt Sally was coming up from the country and was *dying* to see me, I remember looking at her in such disbelief that I had a near out-of-body experience. As I crawled up to my bedroom for the evening (strands of my beautifully coiffured hair doubtless bouncing from the night before), I could not help but wonder how a loving God could really exist if such torment was to be visited upon an innocent child such as I. You can only imagine my view about our Savior at about 9:00 p.m. when I forlornly heard a late-night program on a local radio station, Radio Dublin, playing a request from one young lady, for "John, who can't make Wesley tonight." "But don't worry, John," she signed off, "we will all have a great time for you." Well, will you really? I thought. This was suffering on a biblical scale and I was truly alone in the desert. I was very much reminded of this catastrophic childhood memory when reading 1 Peter the other day when he said that we rejoice when we have to suffer—albeit that was easy for Peter to say as he'd never been prevented from going to Old Wesley.

But of course our suffering and the suffering of others, whether we are young or old, is the distinct and perhaps most abiding debate in our Christian lives and raises its head time and time again. The question is very simple it would appear. If God is a loving God, why does he allow such human suffering? Those two behaviors seem incompatible. Well, I'll let you in on a little secret. That is not an unreasonable question to ask. But when it comes to suffering, the answers for us as Christians are not staring us in the face. Sure, we can talk about the free will that God gave us and that it is we and not he who are responsible for at least most of life's suffering, and that is a reasonable starting point. But it seems, that is all it is. For instance, God makes us very uncomfortable in the book of Job when he appears, on first reading, to provide zero answers to Job's suffering. The problem here is that we have all been trained to use Scripture as a type of divine manual dropped down from heaven. A behavioral code if you will, or like a theological dictionary. The difficulty remains: you can't simply go to the Bible and have a look at Job under "suffering" and get some sort of straight answer. This is even more disconcerting because God appears to allow Job not to just undergo suffering but really *deep* suffering—and what's more, Job of all people absolutely does not deserve it. Sound familiar, anyone?

You will note one thing though. When, for example, Jesus encounters suffering in the Bible he never gets angry with God, but someone else. How does he get there?! Well, Job may actually have a key to our suffering mentioned by the apostle Peter. Job teaches us how to lament and be intolerant of tragedy, evil, and suffering, yet at the same time he advises us to take our confusion, our anguish and despair, and our suffering and pour it all out before God. We must trust in him that the suffering and the pain we are in is in fact the solution to the suffering riddle, and in ways we cannot possibly understand.

Certainly, it is not a solution we can walk away with. We are, after all, a community of apprentices to Jesus. A man who was the crescendo of all the notes of the melody of the Bible, as the wonderful Pastor Tim Mackie says.[1] But that song didn't stop with him. It's still going on. So what it means to be a Christian is to allow our life, with all its suffering, to become another cycle of this melody of the Bible, Mackie advises. Not because we think we can save the world, but because we are pretty sure that we are connected to the one who did. And the only way we can allow him to save us is to take on that tune in our own life stories with all the disappointments and sufferings, and, yes, that even includes Old Wesley disco. So the Bible, and especially Scripture such as the book of Job, becomes our coach and our mentor and gives us the courage to stare into the suffering that is certain for each one of us. After all, Peter says that we rejoice in the certainty of God's salvation, even if now, for a little while, we have to suffer various trials (1 Pet 1:6).

And if we look very carefully we can see that when the night sky shuts down for one last time, it was Scripture that gave us the answers to our pain and suffering all along. As Tim Mackie so eloquently puts it, the Bible gives us the silhouette for all our suffering and Jesus just walks right into it.[2] It's now surely our time to turn on the light.

---

1. Tim Mackie, "The Lost Sermon of Tim Mackie: Discovering the Melody," Ring Them Bells, June 8, 2023, YouTube video, www.youtube.com/watch?v=-7RMbS5Ox3w.

2. Mackie, "Discovering the Melody," https://youtu.be/-7RMbS5Ox3w?feature=shared&t=2520.

Walk On By?

Talking the Talk but Flunking the Walk

PICK A FEW SENTENCES of Scripture. Any sentences. You know, looking across many of them you'd be forgiven for getting a little down in yourself. Let us go to Jeremiah to get the ball rolling: "Why is my pain unceasing, my wound incurable, refusing to be healed? Truly, you are to me like a deceitful brook, like waters that fail" (Jer 15:18). Not a great start to proceedings, we all say. Liven it up, God. But it only gets worse when we randomly flick another Bible page. Paul's Letter to the Romans reads like an unending shopping list of things we need to do for Christ: "Love one another with mutual affection [and] outdo one another in showing honour" (Rom 12:10). Twenty more instructions down the page, he's still at it: more stuff about living in harmony with one another, feeding your enemies, and the like (Rom 12:9–21).

I mean, Paul must surely have known that we are terribly busy people and it's doubtful whether we could find time to fit in *any* of that stuff. What with the kids, grandkids, holidays, back to school, oh, and then there's the golf. Sure, Jesus himself would have been mad for a four ball if he was around today. Then we move somewhere else and that old suffering stuff is back again, and this time Satan is hanging around and we need to get rid of him apparently. (I mean, as if we weren't busy enough with all the other jobs.) All in all, you are probably pretty exhausted, and sure, look, we all just came along to these pages for few nice thoughts. You know, if someone had told you that this part would be all about unending suffering and having to love one another, well, you might have taken a rain check. Anyway, the thing is, we are all really great to each other anyway, so we don't need to be reminded of that. We have buckets of empathy and love. Our problem

Part 1: Reflections from the Shadows

is that we have too much. If only we could be tougher. "Yeah, right," as the young people might say.

In fact, let me now give you an anecdote about how much empathy and concern we all really might have for each other. Picture the scene if you will. It's lunchtime, 1993, in a busy Liverpool Street station, London. Yours truly is having a stand-up lunch in one of the many eateries dotted around the concourse with a work colleague. Three-piece suit, a good salary, galloping thirty-something sincerity, and with ambitions far above his station, this boy here was truly delighted with himself.

Then, from the corner of my eye, I see the bizarre sight of a British rail employee on one of those luggage-carrying toy trains attempting to crash into people as they walk across his pathway. And sure enough, within thirty seconds he has managed to clip an elderly woman who has now fallen to the ground. Cue Spartacus (that would be me), who apparently could take it no longer. With alarming speed considering the sheer volume of haute couture, I soon found myself hurtling across the concourse to stop this wayward rail employee from doing further harm. I do remember thinking at the time, What *exactly* do I do when I get there as, surprising as it may seem, this gentleman is not cut out for fighting, but it was too late. I had committed, and within seconds I found myself hurtling on said gentleman, and instantly we are on the ground and in what I can only assume must have appeared to be an overly vigorous embrace.

Indeed, what passersby must have made of a heavily besuited chap such as I rolling around the ground with a rail employee in an orange boiler suit at lunchtime in one of London's busiest rail stations is anyone's guess. For the record, I am working on the assumption that surprise and pity would have been in the mix. To make matters even worse from a visual perspective, the clearly unwell individual didn't utter a word to me as we spun around the floor like two puppies who had just met. Perhaps this may have been why no one intervened. Perhaps it was because the sight was so bizarre they assumed we must have been making a film. All I can remember is that continued for at least three minutes (think about it: three minutes when two grown men are wrestling with each other, and with no context for anyone who came upon us) and still no one came to my aid. Many had seen the whole tragicomedy playing out, yet still no one intervened. They watched, they laughed (understandably), and some walked away. None came to assist.

Walk On By?

Eventually two Transport Police officers came over and approached me as if I had launched a unilateral attack on a rail employee (in my Sunday best, mind you). The truth soon was revealed, and he was taken away while I brushed myself down, absent my colleague or any bystanders who, by now, had all left. I even saw my sparring partner smiling at me as he was taken away. This really had not been a great lunch. So why did no one come to my aid? What prevented all those people from intervening and helping me (or even my wrestler friend) out? Why did they all stand, with some having their lunch while they were watching, and do nothing to help the situation? One answer, of course, might be it was so entertaining, who would want it to stop? And I do accept that. There is another answer, however, and one beyond all the criminological psychobabble excuses.

It is that none of us really care about each other too much. We might think we care, but we don't really. We might think that deep down we are compassionate people, but the reality is that mostly we behave and act out as if we are not. Of course we think we don't, but that's the old chestnut in academia called "confirmation bias." Or, in other words, it's just us saying it to ourselves and others, and thinking that will be enough. It's not the reality, and we all know this. You see, we might like to think that we are made in God's image so all will be well, but, as I often say, that must surely be a depressing time for God when we start that old self-serving guff. You see, the problem for us is that the Bible's more awkward messages are *for us*. Not some random person over there who doesn't like to sing hymns and say the odd prayer like we do every Sunday. No. All the messages are for us.

Hear these words from Paul: "Love one another with mutual affection; outdo one another in showing honour. Do not lag in zeal, be ardent in spirit, serve the Lord. Rejoice in hope, be patient in suffering, persevere in prayer. Contribute to the needs of the saints; extend hospitality to strangers" (Rom 12:10–13). We need to up our game, ladies and gentlemen. Yours truly, by the way, more than any. We need to stop playing the avatar version of ourselves that simply suits us every day, because that is neither the reality nor the way of our Christian faith. And by the way, no one ever said this faith thing was easy. If you don't believe me, you should have been in Liverpool Street station, one lunchtime, over thirty years ago.

Time to Resolve
To Do Nothing . . .

Recently, I discovered some diaries that I kept as a young boy back in the 1970s. Some of them would make your toes curl. Sorry, all of them. Not least of these was an entry in 1970, when I predicted in April that Ireland would win the FIFA World Cup that year. The fact that they hadn't even qualified for it didn't appear to be an obstacle to my six-year-old self. My Christmas entries were especially bizarre. In 1972, I was hoping that Santa would bring me not one but a number of Chopper bicycles and, wait for it, additionally, and somewhat unremarkably, a Curly Wurly chocolate bar. Once I had reached double digits by 1974, I was becoming more spectacularly realistic for the New Year when I was hoping for not peace in the world, or even Ireland, but only in South County Dublin, would you believe. I must have thought there was terrible gang warfare going on, up and down the local dual carriageway. Typically, though, in the seventies, my New Year's resolutions revolved around giving up chocolate (or, on one occasion, just not eating a specific brand), not fighting with my sister, and, most tellingly, in 1979, aged fifteen, not taking any more of my father's Player's cigarettes without asking him.

Of course I *never* kept to any of my New Year's resolutions, still don't, and probably never will. Or any of my resolutions, come to think of it, and most especially if they are at the beginning or a new year, beginning of term time, just after a birthday, and so on. You all know what I am talking about. The worst time to give up something is when others pressure you to do so rather than yourself. A bit like on Valentine's Day when we are commanded to be all lovey-dovey with one another. Kind of takes the romance out it all, you'll agree? When it comes to our faith, there probably have been times when we have said to ourselves that we need to do more:

Time to Resolve

attend church more frequently, think of God more often, or of loved ones who have passed, and so on. And that's all very well in the aftermath of a turbocharged homiletic. But what about in a couple of hours' or days' time, when the dreary reality and chores of life loom large? Or when we are back in the land of "old clothes and porridge," as my mother-in-law once so succinctly put it.

You see, life has a habit of getting in the way of our faith. I'll give you a moment later, Lord, but I just need to rearrange the sixteen pillows my wife insists on having on the bed. I'll sit down and pray shortly, but first I need to listen to her tell me why it is so important to have all those pillows on the bed. To misquote St. Augustine's most famous line, "Lord make me think of you, but not just yet." I'll be with you, God, tomorrow, we all say, but the problem is (and as the song says) tomorrow never comes. So, in many ways, the times society and then we set ourselves to say that we will immediately draw closer to our faith, might be something of a disaster. It's almost certainly doomed to failure, much in the same way that my childhood hope for peace in the less than rough streets of my area was also doomed to failure. Mainly, in fairness, because the streets were already terrifically peaceful.

No, the time to mend the roof is when the sun is shining, and today may not be the best day for that. But we have made a start by even *thinking* about it. In fact, I am even going to give us a plan. How about you and I from, say, tomorrow say to ourselves that we will go to a quiet room in the house, once a day, for ten minutes max, close our eyes, and do what every secular mind-coach in the world has told us to do. Empty our minds. As people of faith, however, while we are busy emptying it we might also think of restocking it with the wonder of our lives, our short time here on earth, the love we have for others, how we might do better, and that however we do anything we do it in the service of our Maker. It's not going to work all the time, maybe not most of the time—for a few of us, maybe not even at all. But that is not the point. We have made a start and our faith will always do the rest.

And while we sit in the quiet of our own minds and our own souls, we could do worse than have the words of Scripture ringing in our ears when the Lord said to the Israelites via Moses, "The Lord bless you and keep you; the Lord make his face to shine upon you, and be gracious to you; the Lord lift up his countenance upon you, and give you peace" (Num 6:24–26). Faith is never some burden to attend to at Christmas, Easter, weddings, funerals, and maybe other assorted dates during each year. It is not like the few pounds we may have put on, or our lack of exercise. It is, instead, a gift. It is not something to be adjacent to our lives, but something integral to our daily living. So let us do no more than pause for reflection this week as to where we are with Christ and our faith and, when we are ready, then we may start those ten minutes a day. You never know, maybe today will be, after all, a good day to begin.

One thing I can guarantee. Today may be the first day of the week, month, year, or bang in the middle of it all. Of one thing we can, however, be confident, and that is that it is the first day of the rest of your lives. And of that, we can be absolutely certain.

Psycho Killer
Qu'est-ce que c'est?

IN MY LINE OF work, as with all professions, there is always someone who wants to be the best. With offenders it starts something like this: a childhood of abuse and trauma followed by a natural decline into crime—of all sorts. These are the lads (and very occasionally lassies) we call *criminally versatile*, which in English means they will commit any crime, anywhere, because they are always having what we call the L'Oréal moment. That's right—they are worth it. You see criminals are not too different than us. When they qualify within *their* profession, the next question is, How fast they can rise up *their* ladder? After all, there is no point in being a burglar unless you are one of the best, or you'll get caught. There is little point either in being a drug-addled criminal unless you can buy or sell lots of drugs to feed your habit and/or lifestyle and, more particularly, not get caught—in which case you will end of up prison where, you guessed it, you will then try and be the best in-house drug dealer there. Within criminality, there is however consistent talk of a small group of men (and yes, it's almost certainly going to be a man) who seem to fascinate young and old alike, and that is psychopaths.

These are men who are narcissistic, have zero remorse, guilt, or empathy, are impulsive with poor behavioral controls, and are easily bored, needing stimulation from wherever it comes. I know what you're thinking, Madam—"That's my husband." Well you'll be pleased to hear it's almost certainly not, as psychopaths probably account for, thankfully, only about 1 percent of the population. But there is one trait of these disordered men that jumps out at me from Isaiah of all places, would you believe. Let me explain.

Psychopaths have a grandiose sense of self-worth. And, look, I know what you are still thinking: that is definitely my husband; but trust me, it's almost certainly not. (Mind you, I did say *almost*.) These are men who have a grossly inflated view of themselves, with an astounding sense of entitlement, and who trot along life living according to their own, often criminal, rules. But one thing is really striking about them. These men do not wake up each morning thinking they are a star in the universe—they think they are the only star. And that, ladies and gentlemen, is a very, very different proposition.

Which brings me back to Isaiah and how we view or don't view God, and, indeed, ourselves. The Lord says, "I make weal and create woe" (Isa 45:7), which is a frank admission to say the least. No sitting on the fence here. God can be at the heart of suffering and, one assumes, in an uncomfortable way as he can dictate its every turn. And of course the Old Testament can seem to have a habit of describing some of God's retributive behaviors against us as being borderline psychopathic too.

That is if we take the lines out of context, which of course we all almost always do. But let's not do that now. Let's instead read a few lines together for a change. "From the rising of the sun and from the west, [know] that there is no one besides me; I am the Lord, and there is no other. I form light and create darkness, I make weal and create woe; I the Lord do all these things" (45:5–7). Now I don't know about you but that sounds like someone who is in total charge. In other words, in a non-narcissistic way, Christ truly knows he is the only star in the universe. And from time to time we pay lip service to this idea. We glorify Christ, we drop superlatives here and there on a Sunday in our psalms, our readings, and, of course, our hymns. We say to Christ, yes, you are the best, there is no other, nothing else matters. Then, just as quickly, we start swimming around in a phrase we all seem to love—the idea that we are all made in God's image. And then we use that to somehow imagine ourselves to be pretty great too. But wait, doesn't that mean then that we are all stars in the universe and, yes, maybe God's star shines more brightly here and there, but, look, we are all made in his image so we are all kind of similar. Let me suggest that this is our mistake and leads to at best, complacency in our faith, and at worst, complete abandonment.

Apart from the fact that Christ must be holding his head in his hands when he hears us describing ourselves as just like him, think of it in another way. We can't just say the words that God is great, he is almighty, he is powerful as the creator and maker of all things who will lead us all to the new Jerusalem of the book of Revelation. We must actually mean it and act it out in our Christian lives. You see, if we do mean it, it surely leads to us leading the type of lives that he really wanted us to live, not ones where we imagine that God is great, but sure, look, we're not too bad either. Create any story of equivalence with God and we have missed the point. He is it. There is no other. We can enjoy imagining that we are the best architect, or doctor, or sailor, or retiree, or, dare I say it, clergyperson, or lay minister.

I even had an uncle-in-law who used to describe himself as the funniest dentist in Limerick. Which apart from being wrong, seemed to have limited geographical ambition, I think you'll agree. Whether any of these happen to be correct or not, matters not a jot. And if we truly believe they matter, then, we've got a problem. If we truly believe the intrinsic importance of being the best dentist, or flower-arranger, or criminal it's time to get back to Sunday school. In one, very real sense there is *no* equivalence between God and us. We are not all equal stars jostling around the universe, with God occasionally shining a bit more brightly, when we decide it's okay for him to peak ahead of us. There is no equivalence between this nanosecond of our journey that we call life and what came before, and will indeed come after. The problem is if we continue to imagine that how we are in this life is our own doing, and revel in whatever position society has, or, indeed, we ourselves have, put us in, we start to believe that we somehow may be gods in our own right.

The reality is that this notion could not be any further from the truth, for, as John the Baptist says, "The one who is more powerful than I is coming after me; I am not worthy to stoop down and untie the thong of his sandals" (Mark 1:7). Hear those words again. We are not fit to untie the straps of his sandals. The more we can remind ourselves of this fact, the more likely it is that we have understood the story of Christ's journey for us. And, most importantly of all, our glorious and eternal salvation with him.

Judge Not . . .
Taking Positions Is for Yoga Instructors

"Early Saturday, Ciaran was brought to me on a stretcher. I tried to hold him on my best side with total disbelief, none of this made any sense. I spent that night with Ciaran, talking to him and making the most of our final hours together. I spoke to God about Ciaran's favorite toys, food, color, and all the things that made him unique."[1] These were the poignant words of Gillian Treacy in her victim impact statement describing how she lay in hospital beside the lifeless body of her four-year-old boy Ciaran, mowed down by a drunk driver. The death of a child in any circumstances is too difficult for any parent to comprehend. That your child should then have their life ended in so horrendous and criminal a way, simply beggars belief.

As a rule of thumb, the judiciary is generally very good at expressing their horror at violent crime leading to death and serious injury. However, it is said by many that this horror is rarely expressed in the sentence they then subsequently hand down in Britain and Ireland. Some regard it as almost a judicial fashion now to suspend part or, indeed, all of a sentence as if to prove how impressively fair the system is to both victim and offender alike. Sentencing is plausibly based on a desire by a relatively new state, such as Ireland, to show case its liberal criminal justice credentials. Our most serious offense of homicide is a case in point. In 2018, we learned that the average minimum term handed out by Northern Ireland courts for murder was almost ten years lower than in England and Wales, at eleven years and four months.[2] Judges in the Republic of Ireland are also bound by

---

1. RTÉ News, "'My Whole Life Was Shattered, My Heart Was Broken'—Mother of Boy Killed by Drunk Driver," Oct. 27, 2015, www.rte.ie/news/2015/1027/737737-ciaran-treacy.

2. Niall Glynn, "Murder Tariffs 10 Years Lower in Northern Ireland," BBC News NI, Dec. 9, 2018, www.bbc.com/news/uk-northern-ireland-46424942.

Judge Not . . .

the mandatory life sentence for murder, and here the average life sentence for murder was twenty years in 2019, meaning an earlier release date is of course possible.[3] The US? Well that is a very different reflection. More generally, victims of all crime and their families often, it is said, get patted on the head and told to move along so the system can then concentrate on displaying clinical anxiety over the fate of the sex offender, the knife carrier, the murderer, and the child killer. In our rush to present our wonderful humanity to the world, the system has apparently rejected the very people to whom our humanity is most needed. The victims and their families.

Judges have what appears a simple task when considering how they will sentence any particular person. The first is to access the seriousness of the offense and the second is to then consider what circumstances need to be taken into account in order to lessen any possible sentence. So far, so good. Lip service is firstly paid to the seriousness of the offense, and it is slotted into its appropriate category. However, when it comes to mitigating or lessening the possible sentence, the judiciary, some argue, work themselves into a state of high excitement. The mitigation steamroller takes very little time to build up speed and there is nothing the court won't do to try and ensure that the offender spends as little time as is possible in prison. Indeed, convicted persons, it is said, pick up their reward points at a breakneck pace. Have they pleaded guilty to the offense? Yes? Three months off for that act of unrivaled altruism. Little or no previous criminal record? Even better.

In the wrong place at the wrong time? Have two months off for that. What age is the offender? Twenty-one? Their life has just started. A long prison sentence won't benefit them. Sorry, the offender is forty-five? Worse again. They have a family who depend on them financially and emotionally so to put them into prison would ruin more lives. Wait. The offender is in fact seventy-five. What would be the point in putting them in prison with such little time left? That would be an act of unimaginable cruelty. One year suspended.

To the casual observer, the judiciary appears lost. They seem to spend so much of their time bathing in the warm waters of judicial discretion, they appear to have forgotten the one group they are there to protect—the victims. Some believe they live in abject terror of their sentence being ridiculed in a higher court, so they camouflage their judgments on the mercurial grounds of "proportionality" and other jurisprudential gymnastics.

---

3. Cormac O'Keeffe, "'Lifers' Released in 2019 Served Average of 20 Years," *Irish Examiner*, Dec. 1, 2020, www.irishexaminer.com/news/arid-40111037.html.

Part 1: Reflections from the Shadows

Leaving aside the thankless task of the judiciary, nothing is, however, quite as simple as it first appears. This is especially true for those of faith for, "Why do you pass judgement on your brother? Or you, why do you despise your brother? For we will all stand before the judgement seat of God" (Rom 14:10). No one is suggesting, least of all the Bible, that it is not proper that we should organize ourselves in a responsible way where secular judgment is dispensed according to the laws of God. Yet according to judges, it is God and God alone who will not allow sin to go unpunished.

Perspective. Perspective. Perspective. We can rant and rave all we want about the judicial systems we have and the lax or, indeed, draconian sentence practices evident depending on our conservative or "woke" perspective. Some of us may even be talking sense on either side of the debate, but we have missed the point. It is, to quote Ecclesiastes in one very real sense, all *hebel*. Meaningless. Humanity is, after all, not divided between offender and victim, for we are all victims. Victims of our humanity in all its colors and our sin. Victims of crime and their families may be getting a raw deal from criminal justice systems and offenders may appear to be having a better throw of the dice than they may deserve. But, frankly, what is *really* important in all of this? We cannot park the areas of the Christian message we do not like in order to dance around the selective religious lessons that we have fashioned for ourselves. Victims require our Christian respect and love but, equally, so do offenders. This is not a moot point. It is not a topic for reasoned debate for the believer, nor does it languish in the world of "parity of esteem" where all views carry equal weight. We forgive and love all. Because that is who we are. Christians. Period.

To focus our attention, let the words of two people remain in our ears. Gillian Treacy said about her little boy Ciaran who died in the car incident that "he never got the chance to start school, make his Communion, Confirmation, go to college, get married or have children."[4] In a place called Hydebank in Northern Ireland, in a BBC documentary entitled *Boys Banged Up*, one young inmate looked at the camera and said, "My mistake will haunt me for the rest of my life."[5] We embrace Ciaran and this juvenile together, for that is our journey, and let us, in the final analysis, leave the real judgment to he who really knows.

4. RTÉ News, "'My Whole Life Was Shattered."
5. Hannah Price, "Young Offender: 'My Mistake Will Haunt Me for the Rest of My Life,'" BBC, May 2, 2020, www.bbc.com/bbcthree/article/19f93988-7b67-4745-9cc7-459c0de1c5d4.

Making a Criminal?
There but for the Grace of God . . .

SO IT GOES SOMETHING like this. Criminals are not really like you or me. Sure, God love them, they have their burdens and psychological trauma and wouldn't you pity them. Secretly, however, many of us feel that really it's probably nothing a short, sharp kick to the posterior and a good talking-to wouldn't cure. And, now that you mention it, the judicial system is too easy on them, and isn't prison like a luxury hotel for them all? Alternatively, nor can we take too seriously the notion that if we all simply hug it out, coupled with a robust rendition of "Kumbaya," we will somehow decrease the prison population by half. Such recreational tropes certainly have their charms until, of course, they are eviscerated by a group of marauding facts. Christ was, after all, also a pragmatist when it came to compassion.

But first, a spoiler alert. If a parent and/or your community and/or society in general tells you that you are a worthless, violent criminal all your young life, then guess what? You develop what is known in criminology as a "master status." In other words, you become firmly rooted in the very label that has been forced down your throat since birth. The issue then is not that you *are* a violent criminal but whether you can be *the* most violent criminal of your peers. Remember, status anxiety is not just the preserve of boardrooms, law firms, and shop floors. If, on the other hand, like yours truly, you received early family praise to the point of oblivion, chances are you may achieve some modicum of professional success in life (I did say modicum) and likely avoid the clutches of criminality. After all, if you get told you are a superstar for long enough you may just start to believe it, regardless of its veracity. Societal labeling, after all, works for good and for bad. Here's hoping we don't end up in the latter, or we will soon learn what a deviant self-image feels like and how delinquency is then really the only game in town.

Part 1: Reflections from the Shadows

None of this is nuclear physics of course. We learn criminal behaviors as easily as noncriminal ones through our families, our communities, and our society. By virtue of our interactions, or lack of them, with our parents and siblings, intimate personal groups and peers, and our subculture (a pure accident of birth) we make assessments as to whether the legal code is favorable or unfavorable and we act out accordingly. This type of learning in criminology may vary in its frequency, duration, history, and intensity but the fact remains the same. We pick it up as the only way our lives can be lived, and for those born into poverty and desperation it's not difficult to appreciate the likely outcomes.

When those who resort to criminality are mimicking deviant behaviors, suffering catastrophic financial and emotional poverty, and being labeled as the lowest of the low, the rest of us are getting friendly with another criminological conceit, namely social control theory. The real question may be not, why do those bold people over there commit crime but, why do the purest of the pure over here not commit it? Again, another explanation is far less dramatic than we may think. We have attachment to societal norms and values in the same way that criminals do not. For most of us it's worth it to keep the law, to get invested in our communities, and to hold down a family and job. For them it is not. Simple. I told you this wasn't nuclear physics.

Yet before we are finished temporally labeling, corralling, and choking the disenfranchised communities from where the bulk of criminality resides, we pull our greatest trick. We stigmatize them for life and for generations by virtue of what we call in criminology "spoiled identities." That's right, we deeply discredit not only their own very humanity but the humanity of those of their generations who are to come. And many of us still call *them* broken. Are we kidding ourselves? The criminal community may remain outcasts to many of us as we trot along with our astonishingly pedestrian daily woes but, thankfully, not to Christ. They mean more to him than that. Far more. In fact, he even tells us if we help them in life we, too, will have eternal life (Matt 25:34–36). Now before we all go out and start putting ourselves down as prison visitors to guarantee paradise, hold back a moment. Remember all this must come from our hearts and must be real. This is not a variant of Pascal's wager, some sort of third-party fire and theft policy that we should take out just in case it helps us on the far side of the cross.

Making a Criminal?

No, what will help us the far side of the cross is of course accepting that we have already been saved by Christ, and also, importantly, what we do with open and genuine hearts on *this* side of it, too. We are no better than the criminals who we are so fond of boxing off into the "could do better" corner. In fact, we're far worse. The bulk of us had and have all the opportunities. They had and have none. Period. Absent and/or criminal parents, zero familial warmth, childhood trauma, abject poverty, no education, witnessing capricious violence, and often suffering unrecognized childhood brain injury. Is that good enough for a start? Trust me, we could be here all day.

The reality is that the question is not, how come there are so many criminals? Rather, how come there are not so many more? We live a self-serving, secular roller-coaster existence for most of our lives and we do very well to avoid the pit that is crime. One minute we are on top of the world and the next we are in the gutter, courtesy of a family breakup or death, an addiction that has spiraled, or a job that has folded. We are all but one heartbeat away from our very own harrowing of hell that is the streets. But there is one who can save the franchised and the disenfranchised in equal measure. If we let him. Nor is he far away. In fact, he is right in front of us, and he is us.

It's time we cease our silent labeling and stigmatization of those who are in their own lake of fire and choose to save them and who knows—perhaps ourselves in the process.

Heroes and Villains?
Boring!

Now I don't know about you but I am the type of chap who loves to tune into a radio show when there is a good row going. That way I can sit back, tell myself I am great and they are not, and listen to it all unfold. You can only imagine my delight then when I recently heard a cleric on a very popular radio show in Ireland with any number of people lined up to express their horror/delight at the controversial sermon he had preached the previous Sunday. The country appeared to be lined up to have a go, and this show, the nation's conscience, couldn't press the button fast enough to get them on. The cleric didn't seem too bothered, mind you. In fact, he swatted them off with the recreational ease of a man who clearly knew something everyone else didn't. This was radio gold.

Of course radio moments like that don't just happen. They need to have the key elements of an uncomplicated narrative that we all love so much. Depending on your point of view, this was a bad man being grilled by good people or, if you prefer, a good man being grilled by bad people. Take your pick, and anyway it's not really that important where you fall to be honest, for as long as you take part in such radio show extravaganzas you are obliged to line up both heroes and villains in equal measure. And that's that.

Take the Christmas season as an example. This manages to divide us neatly. Apparently, we either love Christmas or loathe it, can't wait for it to start or wish it never had, or cry or laugh at the John Lewis ad. Why does no one say Christmas is "okay"? Why do we always have to become hysterical about it either way? Well, because we just love a bit of envelope-pushing and, trust me, if we can be contrarian, even at Christmas, we will. Not to mention Easter. Of course it was ever so, Christmas or not. Back in the

Heroes and Villains?

day, it was fine (possibly essential), for example, to love Daniel O'Donnell but not so much, for some maybe, the Rev'd. Ian Paisley. The notorious Irish bishop Eamonn Casey suffered the undoubted ignominy of being a great man one minute, then a desperate one the next. Indeed, in reverse, the Rev'd. Ian Paisley himself along with Martin McGuinness of Sinn Fein (another polarizing figure) were eventually to become part of the "chuckle brothers," no less. You see, we are not even too fussed whether you move from loved to hated, and back again to loved, or any combination. As long as we can define you at any single moment as either a national treasure or, indeed, a national disgrace, then all is well. Black-and-white thinking. It makes us all the complete lovable fools we are.

And I do use that technical word *fool* advisedly, for I can't help thinking that Christ must be looking on these radio shows with some wonderment at our general carry-on. He really must also be somewhat disappointed as to how we would all use and reuse his word to demonize certain groups of fellow human beings and, indeed, hero-worship others, because, apparently, the Bible told us so. Well, did it really? You know, I think this may all come as a surprise to God. I mean, even when it comes to the Bible story we have got in wrong with our binary thinking. For example, in the beginning, God created the heavens and the earth. Not the heavens, the earth, and hell. Sorry to disappoint but there is no mention of hell (just yet). However, this is the story many of us still believe because it's, in one sense, easier. Plod along with your life, do your best, and then, all things being equal, you'll head off to heaven, and hopefully not to that subterranean torture-chamber that some of us on radio shows now appear to know so much about. And yes, I know, some of you are saying, hang on. That is exactly what I believe. And that is okay, but it's not the real story.

News alert. Hell is not just somewhere you may or may not go after you die; it's here on earth. It is we who have created it by seizing our autonomy from God, and God wants more than anything (saving your presence) to get the hell out of us. Not just a cleric in Kerry, not Pol Pot, not even just Adolf Hitler, but all of us. And here's a follow on news alert. We have met the enemy already and he is us, and this *is* the Bible story, but it's not as sanitized as the other one we prefer. And why? Because it involves *us all* being responsible for this mess and not simply creating heroes and villains while we shout from the ditch and forget the central characters in this story. Ourselves. Yet we are saved. There is hope. And it is here, right now. At the moment of the cross Jesus allowed the hell we created to overwhelm him and destroy him. In his death, the train wreck of human history is exhausted. Resurrection is his commitment to our good world. A hell-free existence.

So it's not an easy story for us, and its certainly not a binary one. If we therefore consistently park others into the categories of heroes or villains, depict the afterlife as a simple designation of heaven and hell without any reference to this life, describe human personalities as merely good or evil, and then wrap them all up with some loose idea of great *craic* at the end of it all, well . . . we have missed out. So while radio talk shows that demonize may have their charms, their presentation of life's characters is not the *real* story. Instead, we are the tapestry, and when it comes to our human storyboard, much as we may like to create one, there is no black-and-white journeying along the way.

Yet within this more complex picture that we must frame, it is all good news. God is here. God is now. God is forever. Amen to that.

Call Me by My Name . . .
I Am Worthy

THOSE WHO WORK WITH victims of domestic violence advise that often the only thing that strikes you when you enter a shelter for those women who have escaped abusive male partners is the low hum of small children playing. The days of adult laughing and joking have long since departed and in their wake have stepped fear, trepidation, and an extraordinary anxiety. That is what male domestic abusers do. They wholly deconstruct their female partner to a shell of a human. The surprise is not that more women do not leave their abusive partners. The real news story is that any of them do, such is the dismantling of their souls. Abusive men don't just unmake their partners. They eviscerate them.

Of course it is not just men who abuse their female partners. Women, too, abuse their husbands, boyfriends, and significant others. Nor are same-sex partners immune to the horrors of our inhumanity to each other. In the world of the über-domestic abuser, the only common language is violence not gender, and woe betide any partners or family members who may get in their way. A seminal study from the 1990s on domestic violence in the US identified a number of key risk factors for abuse in the home.[1] One or both in the relationship are unemployed, drugs are frequently taken, the man saw the father hitting his mother, the couple are cohabiting not married, are eighteen to thirty years old, are below the poverty level, have a blue-collar background, are both from different religious backgrounds or either uses severe violence toward their children. Two of these factors will mean you

---

1. Richard J. Gelles, "Family Violence, Abuse, and Neglect," chap. 7 in *Families and Change: Coping with Stressful Events*, 2nd ed., ed. Patrick C. McHenry and Sharon J. Price (Thousand Oaks, CA: Sage, 1994).

Part 1: Reflections from the Shadows

are twice as likely to be from an abusive home, compared to if none were present. If you have seven or more, violence is forty times more likely.

Research tells us more. The trajectory of abuse can sometimes be similar across offenders, beginning with degrading behaviors and put downs in public.[2] This can be followed by ensuring the woman (if it is a woman) then becomes entirely financially dependent on the man and money is gifted only at the abuser's behest. And all the while a campaign to prove that the female partner is stupid and worthless continues unabated. By that point the woman is utterly demoralized, disenfranchised, and a hostage, and the physical abuse may not have yet even begun. Then the tension builds further. It can last for days, weeks, months, even years. Verbal attacks increase and the male partner's behaviors become more random and unpredictable. A violent outburst becomes inevitable, and then it appears. Often a savage, atavistic assault on the woman leading to serious physical injuries, from detached retinas to ruptured spleens to broken limbs and jaws, and everything in between. The violence is capricious and excessive and nothing, but nothing, will divert its course.

And so the violence ends and an eerie calm descends amid the physical and emotional destruction. At last now there is peace, both parties will often report to researchers. At least for now the tension has abated and may be interspersed with occasional acts of small "kindnesses" from the abuser, thus reinforcing the view that he is redeemable and this time will definitely be the last. But this is not to be, and for these women the violence never ends. That is, until someone, somewhere, safely gifts them the courage and strength to take their cross and walk to the promised land, where there will be no more torment.

This year and every year will tragically be no different in homes everywhere. While many of us will count our blessings in the warm, loving embrace of family and friends, the homes of these men and women will fill with tears and a paradise that has been truly lost. But where will we be when their trumpet sounds? Will we pretend we did not see or hear their screams in the darkness? Probably. We, too, are broken. As broken as the abused and, indeed, as broken as the abuser. Sure, most of us do not and will not engage in such unspeakable acts, but we are not without sin. That is a given. Yet that is not to excuse the abuser but to understand the rest of us who often inhabit a parallel universe when it comes to even considering

---

2. "Spotting the Signs of Domestic Abuse," Women's Aid, www.womensaid.ie/what-is-abuse.

society's most horrific manifestations. "Tut-tut," we say as we prepare the turkey for Christmas. "Terrible altogether," we say as we attend church in our finery at Easter. Now, if you will all excuse me, I have some important business to attend to. Of course we do...

Certainly there is an awful lot of stuff out there for us to worry about and to try and cure. The Lord will know we are not really cut out for much in the "fixing-things" stakes, especially when it doesn't concern ourselves. But we do have choices to make and lives to help as Christian faithful, whether we like it or not. We can't change the world but we can move a life if we put our mind to it and see what is staring us all in the face day in and day out. Namely, a catastrophic disregard for each other and none more so than in these destructive relationships.

So if you still haven't quite got the horror of domestic abuse, reflect on this. An Irish TV drama of the 1990s "The Family," by Roddy Doyle, is instructive. Its main protagonist and abuser was the pugilistic patriarch Charlo, who uttered the immortal line in one episode, "Chips don't bounce," before unleashing a merciless attack on his wife and children. Those who saw it will never be able to unsee that scene, and that was only drama. Real life can be far worse. Many abused women will report that the one thing they especially remember from the embers of their violent relationship was that their partner never called them by their name. Ever. To do so would, after all, personify that which they are seeking to objectify. Yet all those women ever wanted was their partner to call them by their name. Not names. Their name. And from us, what do they need? Our prayers certainly, but also our actions. Galatians 6:2, after all, tells us that we must carry each other's burdens, and in this way we will fulfill the law of Christ.

We would do well to remember these words when we are having great family occasions, and never forget the reality of what lies beyond the food and alcohol—and try to do something about it. Onward, Christian soldiers.

How Low Can We Go?
Very . . .

THOSE OF US OVER forty years of age may remember. In the lexicon of religious and cultural horrors heaped on the innocent citizens of Northern Ireland over thirty years, this one took the proverbial. Over two decades ago, a picket took hold in the Ardoyne area of North Belfast. During this time, hundreds of "protestors" gathered each morning to hurl abuse at passing children and their parents on their way to school. In a euphemism that we have all come to know only too well on this island, it was benignly described as the Holy Cross "dispute." When a war became "the Troubles," when looting and petrol bombing became "interface tensions," it was inevitable that expletives and even pipe bombs aimed at six-year-old girls on the way to school would be casually labeled a "dispute." In the world of bizarre equivalence, apparently we are all at fault in our own way and if we just give everything a kinder moniker, things won't seem as bad.

When my editor in my newspaper asked me to go to Ardoyne in Belfast and cover the "dispute" for a few days, I expected to encounter a similar situation to that which I had come across before. Two groups of people who, despite their supposed differences, had actually far more kinship with each other than the two countries to which they separately claimed allegiance. What I met, however, was something out of Dante's "Inferno" even by the standards of the "Troubles." The abuse that was thrown at those girls going to school was truly jaw-dropping, and that was only the beginning of it. On the two mornings I walked up the road with some of the families, balloons of urine were thrown at the children, and a few days after I left, pipe bombs were discovered on the route. On my first morning, one of the girls tripped walking on the road. As she lay on the ground, spit rained down on her from a group of men and women baying for blood behind police lines. Their average age I estimated to be about fifty. This was truly biblical. This was calvary.

Let's begin with some very necessary caveats first, though, shall we? That there are two sides to the story in the history of Northern Ireland (or, indeed, any other hot spot in the world) is something of a given. That many from all sides and none should be utterly ashamed of themselves is also somewhat stating the obvious. Politics is by definition nasty, and sometimes very nasty, and we, the poor voters, can occasionally pay too much attention to our elected representatives and start to believe that their dislike of others has some veracity. And that's the harmless enough side of politics where our elected representatives are only human and doing the best with the faculties God gave them. What about the ones who ferment real anger, descent, bigotry, and hatred? What exactly did we do to deserve them and, more importantly, why have some of us taken their lead and behaved like them?

The simple answer for all such behaviors is, of course, that humanity is broken, which, as an explanation for us Christians, is both useful and useless in equal measure. Our brokenness hardly needs much discussion on these pages. It's kind of central to our belief and arguably is the price paid for the free will that has been gifted to us by our God. At the same time, to simply hide behind it to excuse all our aberrant behavior is, to say the least, giving evil a free pass, and this is something we are obliged not to do.

More generally, the problem is further compounded by the fact that our society is anesthetized to hate. My students, for example, no longer ask *why* someone might become a serial killer but who was the *worst*. No more are they horrified by the behaviors of Jack the Ripper and his modern day equivalents, but instead see such behaviors as merely "dramatic" and "fascinating." Our inhumanity to each other is pathological. We, and we alone, are responsible for how we treat each other, and especially our children. There is no political "out" for those middle-aged people who spat on that six-year-old girl while shouting expletives at her, in the same way there is no "out" for any person who would blow up a fish and chip shop on a Saturday afternoon, machine-gun drinkers in a pub, or bomb a Remembrance Day service full of God's innocents—all of which occurred in Northern Ireland.

Yet it's not about "them" or the "other side." It's about us. The Holy Cross terror shamed all humanity as did many other events in Northern Ireland and across these islands over so many years. Yet if we cannot at least treat our children with respect, we may have passed the point of no return, for surely this is one of the key barometers as to what it means to be God's people. But God never leaves us, and even in the pit of despair over two decades ago came Christ's luminous darkness in the perhaps unlikely form of a one Billy Hutchinson of the Progressive Unionist Party. He acknowledged at the time that "the terror on those children's faces was unbelievable" and he was "disgusted to be a loyalist" having seen what he did.[1] He suffered abuse from his own people for these words, but he had merely expressed what the whole country had felt, of whatever religious hue. The line had been crossed. Full stop.

Yes, it may be true that every time we suffer, every time we experience evil, we may grow in a peculiar way as God's children, but that can never be our excuse to perpetrate evil on a child, or any human, or sentient being. So, as we see our children and our grandchildren enjoying their respective schools in relative safety across the world, let us never forget what we were capable of on the island of Ireland over two decades ago and start to reignite a bit more of that love and compassion thing we hear about every Sunday in all our churches. In the final analysis, don't, however, take my word for it. Ill treatment of children, regardless of our own interpretation of the political certitude of our behaviors at any given time, remains heinous, for we may "not despise one of these little ones" for "in heaven their angels continually see the face of my Father in heaven" (Matt 18:10).

Carl Jung may have been right all along. We all may miss God because we fail to look low enough. Time to get down on our knees.

---

1. Louise McCall, "Billy Hutchinson 'Disgusted to Be a Loyalist,'" *Irish Independent*, Sept. 5, 2001, www.independent.ie/irish-news/billy-hutchinson-disgusted-to-be-a-loyalist/26073209.html.

Do You Want to Be in My Gang?
Of Course I Do . . .

THERE'S NOTHING QUITE LIKE being in a club or any band of like-minded individuals. All the angst and worry that surround whatever sporting, yachting, political, social, or cultural interest is your thing drift away as you subsume your soul to the collective. Sure, we can't *all* be wrong, can we? Certainly, the idea of "coalitional psychology" has its charms. Research suggests that men are genetically predetermined to form groups due to our biosocial mission to achieve resources and protect the group.[1] And to think you never knew, ladies. And boy (pun intended) do we love to form groups. Initially we may have designed these for hunting activities but now we form groups of football fans, closed men-only clubs, religious, and, of course, militant groups. The truth is, if we notice another man walking down the street, we are tempted to introduce him to a draft constitution we prepared earlier. I mean there must be something we can join, we say.

Unsurprisingly, perhaps, I am that coalitional soldier. Generations of the family have been wedded to Liverpool Football Club for no discernible reason other than it's only a hundred-mile swim away from Dublin. Yet, trust me, it is an out-of-body moment. Singing "You'll never walk alone" at the Kop end of Anfield with your son on one side of you, a urologist on the other (I kid you not), and an elderly man behind us throwing around stolen chunky Kit-Kats has few rivals. Former Liverpool manager and legend Bill Shankly hit it on the nail when he said, "Some people believe football is a matter of life and death, I am very disappointed with that attitude. I can

---

1. Marc Kay, "What's Wrong with Being Wrong: A Closer Look at Evolutionary Ethics—Part 2," *Journal of Creation* 36:3 (Dec. 2022) 92–98, https://dlo.creation.com/articles/p157/c15745/j36_3_92-98.pdf.

Part 1: Reflections from the Shadows

assure you it is much, much more important than that."[2] He was, of course, correct. It is about "living"—wherein can lie moments of pure epiphany when (and with more than a nod to Matt 2:10) we see the stars, and rejoice exceedingly and with great joy.

Research suggests a different coalitional manifestation for women who do not have the same aggressive and defensive motivation that men exhibit, and it appears they have a greater degree of hierarchal discrimination than their male counterparts.[3] This all sounds very wise, and with all the usual cognitive balance we might expect, until we realize what this really means is that women prefer to establish social relationships with other women of the same social status, avoiding those they perceive to be of lower status. Think book and bridge clubs. The fact that women may be less tolerant of each other in terms of hierarchal stratification means coalitions for them are less frequent and can arguably set females at a social disadvantage compared to their male counterparts.

Yet does it? A world away from football and book clubs lies the darker side of male coalitional psychology where "in groups" and "out groups" are created amid a febrile certainty. While we all look for cognitive closure in our lives, the need to be assured about the future, for many, due to social, cultural, political, and economic circumstances, this is not possible. The disenfranchised young men of Syria and Iraq, for example, are so reduced, and into this social milieu arrives ISIS with the promise of cognitive closure and a personal significance on this earth and in heaven. All these men must do is adopt black-and-white thinking, with no shades of gray. In this corrupt vision, the world is only populated with saints and sinners, heroes and villains, order and chaos, Islam and infidels. A terrible, dehumanized "out group" is then created whom are little more than a product to be disposed of at will. Essentially, a moral license has now been granted to slaughter. And of course the bankruptcy of militant coalitional psychology by so-called Christianity has also been laid bare in recent years. Think the extermination of the Jews by "Christians" during World War II. Think also the slaughter at Srebrenica in 1995 when eight thousand Bosnian Muslim men and boys were genocidally massacred by the (Orthodox) Serbian army under the indifferent glare of UN (potentially Christian) peacekeeping forces.

2. "Commemorate the Anniversary of Shankly's Death with 25 Incredible Quotes," Shankly Hotel, Sept. 25, 2018, https://shanklyhotel.com/bill-shanklys-best-quotes/.

3. Nerisa Dozo, "Gender Differences in Prejudice: A Biological and Social Psychological Analysis" (PhD thesis, University of Queensland, 2015), https://doi.org/10.14264/uql.2015.777.

Do You Want to Be in My Gang?

When it comes to militant "clubs," we of all faiths and none have evidenced truly despicable human traits.

On a lighter note, nor was Jesus a stranger to the phenomenon of the "group." The Bible is replete with stories of crowds, groups, and "clubs" getting together for good, neutral, and, indeed, evil purposes. In truth, in the Synoptic Gospels of Matthew, Mark, and Luke, you would probably need to set up a support group for a chapter that doesn't tell of a crowd following Jesus, gathering near him, or at least getting together to discuss him. Myriad "collectives" were evident in Jesus' time such as the Pharisees and Sadducees whose relentless questioning prompted him at one point to say, "Woe to you, teachers of the law and Pharisees, you hypocrites" (Matt 23:13 NIV). He wasn't far wrong. If you want to locate galloping smugness and collective certitude, look no further than the oftentimes bizarre groupings and coalitions we as humans can form.

It is also true that there are certainly times when we need to get away from the clubs, coalitions, and crowds and, like Jesus, find our own boat and go to a secluded place by ourselves (Matt 14:13). Indeed, this is surely paramount if we are to get to know our God. However, we may also still find joy in banding together in all our clubs and societies and on a Sunday when we gather with those past and present and those to come as a communion of saints to listen to his word. We may hazard a guess as to what our God thinks of those of us who gather together and form militant groups to massacre others in the name of nothing, for "You shall not follow a majority in wrongdoing" (Exod 23:2). What he thinks of our benign clubbing together is another matter, although I suspect he might approve. Whether our lives are flashing before us in the Kop at Liverpool Football Club, while playing a four-ball with friends, delivering the perfect hand at bridge, or worshiping together in our churches, the joy of joining together in unity for the glory of his name can never be underestimated.

Leaving church aside, perhaps Groucho Marx was right all along. I mean who of us would want to join a club that would have us as a member? Indeed, as we form, leave, and disband clubs, groups, and coalitions during our lives, let us remember that the final great gathering is perhaps all we have to truly consider when we will behold a great multitude which none of us can count, "standing before the throne and the Lamb" (Rev 7:9).

Jimmy Savile
Hiding in Plain Sight

In October 2012, a police operation in Britain, code named Operation Yewtree, began to investigate sexual abuse allegations made against a group of so-called celebrities.[1] They were common household names: Jimmy Savile, Rolf Harris, Stuart Hall, and Fred Talbot—to name but four. Further police operations were instigated such as Operation Hydrant where 261 men of "public prominence" were investigated. The public looked on in apparent shock as the list of those being scrutinized for allegations of child sexual abuse climbed ever higher and their reported alleged deeds became even more shocking.

Operation Yewtree did more however than lift the lid on men who had abused and destroyed innocent lives. It went further than simply bringing a significant number of these men, both unknown and unknown, before the law courts to face their temporal punishments. It even did more than reveal astonishing levels of, at worst, collusion and, at best, cover-up from the BBC to certain NHS trusts and beyond. Most of all, it shone a full arc light, not simply on the closed institutions and secret clubs of that era, but, far more worryingly, on another group. The general public who, whether we liked it or not, were a part of this terrible tapestry. Let us not put too fine a point on it. If that generation were to advise young people today that the biggest male celebrity on British TV some forty years ago openly admitted that he was "feared in every girl's school in this country" and that there was no need to "chase girls" because he had "thousands of them on Top of the Pops,"[2] that generation would simply not be believed. That no atten-

---

1. Wikipedia, "Operation Yewtree," last modified Jan. 9, 2025, https://en.wikipedia.org/w/index.php?title=Operation_Yewtree&oldid=1268296083.

2. Wikipedia, "Jimmy Savile," last modified Jan. 6, 2025, https://en.wikipedia.org/w/

tion would be given when the same individual also advised that "tabloids were sniffing around him" for salacious stories and so it was an "enormous relief" when he "got the Knighthood," would also be disbelieved.

In case we had not gotten the message that he was abusing children and adults he made further public announcements. "Women know too much. I'm all for girls that don't know too much,"[3] he opined on countless occasions. This same man abused a young girl live on television and was well known to be a sex offender in his and related circles, and yet still he remained very close with senior politicians and, indeed, royalty. It was even reported that one senior royal sought his advice on a range of matters, not least so that they might understand the hearts and minds of the ordinary British public.[4] Savile's public commentary about men, women, and children was entirely inappropriate, even by the dubious attitudes existing at that time. He could barely string a coherent sentence together unless he had cue cards in front of him, and his entire professional life rested on mindless catchphrases, a lurid dress sense, and an uncanny ability to court and enjoy public adulation. He appeared disengaged, disinhibited, at best narcissistic, and at worst psychopathic. Yet still he was described and regarded by all as a quintessential British "character."

He was of course anything but; rather this a man who abused up to a thousand victims of all ages,[5] ruining countless other innocents along the way. How did he do it? In full view. Jimmy Savile hid in plain sight for his entire life and either no one noticed who or what he was, or everyone was in too much awe of his celebrity and charity work to do anything about it. After all, this man built hospitals and no one appeared prepared to believe that he would at the same time also destroy lives. Additionally, he was a man of faith, and we know this because he told us so on countless occasions and even managed to ingratiate himself with the then-pontiff. Jimmy Savile walked on water and he wasn't about to drown. Yet for every hero this generation created like Savile, it also created its antiheroes. And who better a person to villainize than Johnny Rotten, lead singer of the Sex Pistols and

---

index.php?title=Jimmy_Savile&oldid=1267665179.

3. "Jimmy Savile Quotes," IMDb, www.imdb.com/name/nm0767675/quotes.

4. Kevin Rawlinson, "Prince Charles Repeatedly Sought Jimmy Savile's Advice, Documentary Claims," *Guardian*, Apr. 6, 2022, www.theguardian.com/uk-news/2022/apr/06/prince-charles-repeatedly-sought-jimmy-savile-advice-documentary-claims.

5. Daniel Boffey, "Revealed: How Jimmy Savile Abused up to 1,000 Victims on BBC Premises," *Guardian*, Jan. 18, 2014, www.theguardian.com/media/2014/jan/18/jimmy-savile-abused-1000-victims-bbc.

Part 1: Reflections from the Shadows

bête noire of the British tabloids and family values. Vilified by middle Britain, he was presented as nothing short of the new antichrist, the destroyer of faith, the harbinger of satanic values. If Jimmy Savile was the biblical Moses, then Johnny Rotten was its King Herod. After all, this generation was expert at delineating between good and evil, right?

Nothing could be further from the truth. Christ gave this generation a challenge and, like so many other times, we failed him abysmally. Johnny Rotten (real name, John Lydon) spoke out publicly about the known behaviors of Jimmy Savile and others and he was ignored, if not ridiculed further. As far back as 1978, Lydon was banned by the BBC for speaking out on Savile when he called him a "hypocrite,"[6] all the while Jimmy Savile et al. rose higher in the public imagination. It is a cruel irony of who we are that those we praise can display the worst aspects of humanity and yet those we choose to pour scorn on, can often be the finest examples of Christ's love. The Savile/Lydon dichotomy is not just a tale for the ages, it is also a tale that we as Christians learn from Scripture. How many times does Luke tell us to love our enemies? Why were we not able to do that with our supposed cultural enemy John Lydon? Far more worryingly, why were we so capable of idolizing and, so by default, ensuring the appalling behaviors of Jimmy Savile?

It is not good enough to smugly start switching the narrative over the last number of years since Operation Yewtree. Where were we when victims needed us? Why did we not listen to Lydon and a few others when they told us what, apparently, everyone knew? Lydon was the biblical Joab or Zacchaeus and if not hated was at the very least held in contempt by many of that generation. Savile, on the other hand, achieved Abrahamic status in that specific cultural milieu. Humanity really has a lot to learn when it comes to recognizing good and evil. And our biggest challenge of all in this terrible story? It is not only that we must love those we perceive as our enemy, such as John Lydon back in the day. We must also love those who were our heroes and who have now fallen immeasurably, such as Jimmy Savile. The message is simple, remember. Christ loved "bad" people. Can we? In the final analysis, we might begin by being more alert to the places where good and evil reside and recognizing that both can be found in the strangest places. Not least in us.

---

6. Guardian Music, "John Lydon Says He Was 'Banned from BBC' over Jimmy Savile Comments," *Guardian*, Sept. 24, 2015, www.theguardian.com/music/2015/sep/24/john-lydon-says-he-was-banned-from-bbc-over-jimmy-savile-comments.

Smooth Criminals
"Meaningless" Is a Movable Feast

CRIMINALS GET A BAD rap. In fairness, in one sense, it's well deserved. There go the poor fools of the globe working day and night to keep a roof over their heads, food on the table, and clothes on their children while these men (and occasionally women) play fast and loose with societal norms and yet still manage to get by on state handouts and ill-gotten gains. Meanwhile, we non-criminals (for the avoidance of any doubt, a great bunch altogether) are plodding away, fighting the good fight, and finishing the race, if you will. Criminals, on the other hand, may be fighting the good fight all right, although somewhat literally; and as for finishing the race, well, they are already at the finish line before you've even taken off. It's called cheating. So they are just terrible people and, while the rest of us are not all good, we do our best and, in any event, we are most certainly better than them. It's a fairly simple binary position, and, on one level, it makes some sense. Criminals obviously do bad things, while non-criminals do not. But there's a problem. Anyone, now for the last tired trope?

And this trope isn't just tired. It's exhausted. While black-and-white thinking has its charms and allows us to set up a childish battle of good and evil in our worldviews, life has other ideas, especially when it comes to its true color—gray. We have no biblical indications as to Christ's favorite shade but I am quite sure it could possibly have been a gunmetal or charcoal gray, for nothing is ever as it seems, or as we want it to be. It's all very well being angry or dismissive of the assaulter, or house burglary, or rioter, or street drug addict, but here is a criminological secret: they did not choose this life, rather it chose them. That is not to say that they are not capable of choices, because they are. The problem is the vast majority just don't have any and/or don't know how to make them. The rest of us all made sure of that despite their collapsing social environments, even worse home lives (if they have any), plus zero love and affection from any individuals or communities. Top that with endemic poverty and a genetic predisposition to believe that the world is against them (because it is) and we've got a problem. To finish off this recipe, we then throw in a bit of old-fashioned name-calling where, regardless, we label them and their families *criminals* by our words and actions. Criminology secret number two: label someone, something for long enough and, guess what, they may just become it. The real wonder is therefore not that we *have* criminals. Rather, how is it we don't have far more?

Christ's view of the downtrodden and disaffected is all over Scripture. Indeed, it *is* Scripture. We all know this, apparently, but sometimes it may be more instructive to think outside the notion of simply remembering those who are in prison (Heb 13:3) or chattering among ourselves about justice for the poor (Ps 140:12). These are mere words, or as the book of Ecclesiastes might have called them, *hebel*—something that is "meaningless," like a puff of wind. Indeed, our on/off relationship with those we may sometimes see as less than ourselves has powerful if hidden resonance in Ecclesiastes. This book asks all the questions of life's miseries but can, to many, fail to provide any answers. It has been described as the biblical "desert sphinx" raising inconsistencies and contradictions—all of which go unexplained by the author in equal measure. Even Martin Luther thought that it was a work that no one ever has really mastered.[1] Some have even wondered whether it should be in the Bible at all, such is its apparent pessimism.

Now I doubt very much that any criminals on a theft spree up and down any country will be giving too much thought to the horrors of the philosophizing of its author, Qoheleth. In fairness to them, they are too busy surviving. The rest of us don't have that excuse though. So what can we, the chattering masses, take from it when it comes to our attitudes to the downtrodden, the abused, the prisoner? Ecclesiastes is very concerned with the apparent futility of human existence so that no less than thirty-seven times do we hear the word *hebel*. This word has been described as whatever you are left with after you burst a soap bubble. That's right. Nothing. Unfortunately the poor author of Ecclesiastes is continually tortured by what he sees as life's meaninglessness. The author considers a range of other

---

1. David E. Prince, "Introduction to the Ecclesiastes of Solomon: Martin Luther," Prince on Preaching, June 9, 2018, www.davidprince.com/2018/06/09/introduction-to-the-ecclesiastes-of-solomon-martin-luther.

issues relating to man's existence such as political power, the accumulation of wealth, sizable families, and a prolonged life. All the stuff we love. Unfortunately, he comes to the same answer. The *fact* of death and general human powerlessness will inevitably render everything, he says, "meaningless."

Certainly, there are times in our lives when we will feel such a sense of utter hopelessness for that, after all, is our broken, human condition. A lot of the time, though, we genuinely think our lives are meaningful, but for all the wrong reasons. Think for a moment about the criminal who steals your mobile phone, attacks you or your family, or otherwise creates mayhem in your life. Hard to feel sorry for them, right? Yet the criminal finds it hard to feel sorry for you, too. Some of your life may feel meaningless but, remember, all of their life is. For them, there is no hope, ever. Now, if the criminals could just put down their jemmies for one moment, the central question raised by Ecclesiastes on life's futility would doubtless hurt them, but, then again, they probably know more about life's hurt than you or I.

The truth is that Ecclesiastes should really awaken the rest of us. This book pulls back the curtain and says that the myth of religious fulfillment reverses the gospel. Why? Because it says our lives are not all about us inviting God into our story but him inviting us into his. Yet before we can accept his invitation we must go to him with open hearts and without anger toward anyone, especially those who do us and others criminal wrongs. How about we therefore try to make our own lives *meaningful* and in the process improve theirs? It's just a thought. In the meantime, let all us self-appointed "decent" people remind ourselves that it is not our business to live in the sins of criminals. After all, we should be busy enough living in our own. Rather, our job is to understand and feel compassion for them, as we do the victims of crime. Regardless, and as Ecclesiastes advises, when everything is *hebel*, the only thing that is left is faith in the Lord. And when it comes to faith, remember that word is for everyone.

Part 2
The Seven Deadly Sins

Wrath
Hold Me Back. Please.

O NE OF MY DOGS, Louis, is big. Very big. One hundred ten pounds of Newfypoo—of furry, Irish, Newfoundland cross, with the emphasis on cross. You see Louis isn't happy when he encounters scooters, bikes, children, other dogs, cats (oh, does he hate cats), sheep, rodents, and those he perceives to have any outstanding arrest warrants. Oh yes, and one other group: humans. So all in all, he spends most of his time being angry, except maybe when he's at home and even then he gets a tad wrathful if you don't rub his chest for an hour at a time. Cross by name, cross by nature, Louis appears to be a large angry ball of fur for whom life has dealt some incredible challenges.

Of course he's not. Wrathful, I mean. He is however very nervous, and I am not just saying that to explain away the canine equivalent of Hannibal Lecter. He's not angry with everything; he is actually terrified of everything, and most especially himself. After all, there are not many dogs who will whimper with terror and awe when they accidentally break wind. So Louis is just plain, old-fashioned scared of everything. Think the Lion in *The Wizard of Oz* but stuck on a ghost train. On a loop. Okay. You're getting there. So imagining that Louis and certain of his doggie compatriots are either angry or wrathful in nature may be to somewhat miss the point. A bit like all of us, really. Angry men are all the rage these days (see what I did there?), and I come in contact with them all the time. Before me in the magistrates' courts in the UK, sitting on the other side of a criminological research table, in prison, on the streets, and, yes, in the boardroom. Anger is sadly, the new "love."

What exactly are we all so rageful about though? I wonder. Men seem particularly unhappy and keep having to go to war to prove how angry they are and sort out yet another perceived injustice. Anger has become like a first language for many and not to get angry can be seen as some fashion of weakness, for injustice lies everywhere and we men must right it. In fairness, it wasn't off the ground we licked it. Sure there are angry lads are all over the Bible. Cain killed Abel of course; Levi and Simeon angrily destroyed a city; Saul attempts to kill David in a pique of anger; and Jonah brings passive aggression to a new level with gold-standard pouting when God dares to spare Nineveh. Even Moses manages to get into this anger thing, so frustrated is he by the people of Israel. I mean, even Christ himself was known to lose his temper here and there; and God the Father spends a significant amount of time in the Old Testament apparently showcasing his ire, vengefulness, and wrath. Come to think of it, you might need to set up a support group for those in Scripture who don't do wrath.

But the repackaging of anger today as some sort of noble and necessary righteousness has perhaps reached new levels. Ukraine is angry with Russia and Russia is vengeful toward Ukraine. Israel and Palestine are angry with each other and wish to unleash merciless wrath (but righteous, of course) on the other. Protestants hate Catholics and Catholics hate Protestants; certain branches of Islam hate Judaism and seek to destroy it while certain parts of Islam hate . . . well . . . certain other parts of Islam. And, by the way, chopping selected passages from the Old or New Testament out of context to support righteous anger won't help us either. It kind of never does.

To a greater or lesser extent, anger is the new black and today we all feel wrathful toward each other fairly consistently, and that all appears to be fine. Why? Because our anger is more righteous than ever before. Funny the way anger is now always righteous. Not only that, it's a lifestyle choice, and those people, especially men, who are either incapable or unwilling to express righteous anger at some point in their lives are somehow seen as lesser. The difficulty is that our personal sin can light our own anger like few others. Giving it the catwalk moniker of "justified anger" does not make it is so. It just means we have window-dressed it. Sorry to disappoint but that is not the same thing. Christ gave us free will and that was his gift to us. Our thanks is to abuse the trust and hope he placed in us by behaving like the angry, frightened humans we are. Yet he could not be any clearer on the futility of wrathfulness. "Let everyone be quick to listen, slow to speak, slow to anger, for human anger does not produce God's righteousness" (Jas 1:19–20).

Wrath

We tend to forget that one when we are screaming at our partners or children, disparaging anyone who may deviate from our world view, placing bombs in cars, invading countries, or executing others who might not share our faith. Righteous wrath is the greatest con job we humans have ever pulled, but the joke remains firmly on ourselves. Christ recognizes our anger, but he has a solution. Hold the wrath. "Be angry but do not sin; do not let the sun go down on your anger, and do not make room for the devil" (Eph 4:26). His answer according to Pastor Brad Archer? The Psalms. "Search me, O God, and know my heart; test me and know my thoughts. See if there is any wicked way in me, and lead me in the way everlasting." (139:23–24).

Anger and wrath remain the animals crouching at the door of every human and yet still we leave that door unlocked. We desperately try to convince ourselves and others that our anger and savagery are nothing of the sort and are instead justifiable behaviors where an "injustice" has been done to us. Now call me a bluff, old traditionalist, but haven't we all missed the point here? If anger is always about being scared (which it always is in some way) it would appear that we are all a bunch of nervous pooches walking around the place trying to look tough when all we really want to do is to burst into tears and get a nice, big hug. Louis included.

So time for us to park our anger and let out the true emotion, for Christ will be there to hold us when we falter.

Pride
Goes Before You Know What

P RIDE GOETH BEFORE DESTRUCTION and a haughty spirit before a fall says Prov 16, which admittedly may not be cheeriest note on which to begin a deadly sin. Indeed, that old "pride before a fall" malarkey sounds like something of a blast from the past for most us, I'm guessing. In Belfast, were you to hear a mother berating a child for being prideful, chances are someone would call the language police. In Dublin, they might actually call the police. Pride sounds so yesterday (as the young people might say), and in this new land of the boastful and the free, the one-eyed social media monster is king, and it would most certainly never regard pridefulness as being a negative. Rather a core component of self-help.

The following may instruct, however. Before making my confirmation, I remember badgering my parents into getting me a pair of linen trousers. I must have looked some sight in church that day and doubtless the congregation must have assumed that I had strayed away from the zoo. But to me, all that didn't matter. I had linen pants and the rest of my peers did not. In my own simple, little head, that made me better than them. This somewhat pointless, and comically prideful journey, continued during my early life. When I got into the workplace, for example, I was delighted with myself when I got promoted. Being promoted meant you were rising up the ladder and in the process, of course, leaving the "unpromoted" behind you. That was great altogether. Great, that is, until you met someone who had a better title or job than you. I remember working for Barings Bank in London (that was the one that was collapsed by the infamous Nick Leeson, by the way) and getting promoted to the grand title of "Head, Debt and Derivatives." To this day I am not entirely sure what that really meant but it didn't matter. My business card said I was "Head, Debt and Derivatives," so

Pride

that meant I was important. Important, of course, until a week into the job when I was introduced to the "*European* Head, Debt and Derivatives." As you can imagine, I was gutted. From hero to zero in one handshake. Now my eyes were firmly set on the European head's title, as that had my name written all over it. Until, of course, I was then to meet the "*Global* Head of Debt and Derivatives." Pride doesn't just come before a fall. It comes before meeting the "Global Head" of anything.

And dare I say it, it is not just myself. You, too, all know what I am talking about. In your professional lives, also, you were, and, indeed, maybe still are, delighted with any promotions or successes that came along. After all, more money, more status, and a new business card. Could life get any better? Of course not. Those of you who worked or work as homemakers, too, even have your own pecking order, be it in terms of the control of the organization and administration within the home, or perhaps on the board of the local school. Or maybe you aspired to be lead actor in the local amateur dramatics society? Albeit you only ever ended up being a stagehand with the odd cameo role. The retired, too, keep it up, in different ways of course. Chairperson or mere secretary of the residents' committee? Sweet soloist or general grunter in the church choir? Or perhaps you are an assistant in the local charity shop but really have your eye on the main prize; that of manager.

You see, when it comes to pecking orders we just love them. If we were being honest our time spent on this earth is entirely wrapped up, to a greater or lesser extent, earning and working toward *advancement*, whether it be in our jobs, in our homes, in our communities, and, yes, maybe even in our churches. Which brings me to Nicodemus in the Bible. This man gives the impression of someone to be reckoned with. In some places it might even have been commented that if he was a bar of chocolate, he would have eaten himself. He was after all a member of the Ruling High Council of the Jews, and one of their tasks was to investigate false prophets—a bit like a theological audit, but ultimately an act which clearly says: "I am able to judge you." Now don't get me wrong. Nicodemus was respectful toward Jesus. He calls him "Rabbi" and says he is a great teacher. A bit like the way we might speak of those who might be in our employ, or to whom we may be a boss. Respectful, but we still believe that we have advanced to a place above them.

But Jesus is up to this notion that we can all earn our prideful place through hard work, and so speaks to Nicodemus's compliment, somewhat abruptly. He says he must be "born again" to enter the kingdom. It wasn't good enough for them to live their lives according to the strict rules of the scribes. Simply sticking to the law and following Abraham so that their place in heaven might be secure was missing the point (John 3:1–21).

The problem is that entrance into God's kingdom has nothing to do with our alleged good works, our promotions, our positions, our ethnicity, our ancestry, or the latest addition to our CV. That's all about that pride stuff (trust me, I know). None of us can earn a place in God's kingdom with our so-called achievements, professional accomplishments, or by advancing our societal status. To make matters worse, when we harvest these accomplishments we then become prideful. Jesus says Nicodemus must be born again and washed by water and the Spirit. In plain English he is telling us that we should treat any type of worldly achievements as exactly that, worldly only, temporary.

God's response to you or me when we do well in our career? Emm . . . so what? Doing *badly* in our professional lives? Same response. The truth is that when all the CVs have been put away, all our taxes have been paid (or not), all the golf clubs joined, and the retirement funds spent, we are left with one central question. Are we primarily prideful or prideless?

To bring the tone down again, the problem is that we all come in and go out of this world the same way. On our own. However, with Christ there is always good news, once we choose to accept it. If we turn to face God now and truly realize that what only matters is love and compassion for each other, and so him, then it is he who will hold our hand on that day and walk with us to his promised land. Pride isn't interested in Christ's love and compassion, and, in any event, won't be much use to us on our final journey.

And who knows? Christ may even give a look to those who wore silly linen trousers.

Greed

Who Ate All the Pies? We Did . . .

"**G**REED." A REALLY GREAT word, and frankly not used enough anymore. The most underrated of the seven deadly sins in my view. The *Oxford Dictionary* advises us that greed is a "strong desire for more wealth, possessions, power, etc. than a person needs" or, "a strong desire for more food or drinks when you are no longer hungry or thirsty."[1]

Let's be honest, though, most of us think of the latter description. A fool like me eating his bodyweight in chocolate in the corner, and, trust me, I don't need Easter for that to occur. "Will you look at the big greedy head on you?" was once roared at me by my principal in school as I ate my way through the crusts of other boys' lunch boxes when they had "finished." When I was a kid, if you moved, you became a legitimate culinary target. Didn't matter what or how much I ate in those days, I still looked like an anxious whippet. Now, I just look anxious.

At the same time, we have all now apparently decided that greed has become somewhat diluted as a "sin," if we even think it is one at all. Today greed is regarded as a mere lapse into temptation (let he who is without a large packet of sweets, cast the first chocolate egg, etc.) and, sure, nothing that can't be corrected by a weekly weigh-in at Slimming World in the community center. Mind you, Scripture hasn't forgotten or relegated greed, though, even if we have. In fact, it mentions greed of all hues upward of seventy times, and, yes, it does even mention the seemingly harmless enough gluttony variation of greed. Indeed, Proverbs goes large (pardon the pun) on it all. Without putting too fine a point on it, "If you have found honey, eat only enough for you, or else, having too much, you will vomit it" (Prov

---

1. *Oxford Advanced American Dictionary*, "Greed," Oxford Learner's Dictionaries, https://www.oxfordlearnersdictionaries.com/definition/american_english/greed.

25:16), or, somewhat more disturbingly, "When you sit down to eat with a ruler, observe carefully what is before you, and put a knife to your throat if you have a big appetite" (23:1–2). I know. A quick visit to McDonald's with your boss will never quite be the same again.

Having said that, it wasn't just Solomon and friends in Proverbs who had it in for gluttony. Even Eliphaz said to Job (a man who was busy giving a whole new meaning to suffering) that, "because [the wicked] have covered their faces with their fat, and gathered fat upon their loins, they will live in desolate cities" (Job 15:27–28). Think carefully, therefore, before you have that next Cadbury's or Hershey's. Yet surely all of this has got to mean something more than simply trying not to stuff your face with bars of chocolate. Yes, it does mean something, and something far more. Something indeed that goes to the heart of who we are as Christians.

Herewith, a seemingly innocent case of greed. As a boy attending one of the country's favored rugby-playing schools, I managed to only ever play one competitive game, which was an achievement in itself. My greed, however, for that one match was awe-inspiring. I decided that I could play both wing and wing-forward at the same time, and in my world it was the least I deserved. The confusion for both teams was worth the watch as a slight child appeared to be involved in any scrum, maul, back, or forward position that he so chose. I danced around that pitch like Billy Elliot. After all, I was a lover not a fighter and this was *my* match. In an understandable reaction to my greed and selfishness, my own captain punched me in the ribs on the way off the pitch at the end of the match just to show me what he thought of me, only to be followed moments later by the referee who barged me to the ground in a fit of frustration. Billy had truly danced his last rugby pirouette, and really had no one to blame but himself.

And this is the problem with greed. What seems like a relatively innocuous part of the human condition, and at times laughable, is in fact nothing of the sort, especially when we start evidencing this trait as adults. You cannot serve God and money says Matt 6:24 in a moment of unrivaled clarity. And it's not just ourselves who will be affected by our insatiable greediness; greed monsters will even bring ruin to their own households (Prov 15:27). Indeed, Scripture never ceases to remind us that our greediness will be our ultimate fall. Because, guess what? We took nothing into the world and we will take nothing out, and if we want to get worldly "rich" (in whatever way we imagine this "richness") then we will be plunged into ruin and destruction (1 Tim 6:6–9).

Greed

Of course none of us really like this biblical message so we reinvent it to suit the new descriptor of greed being more like "legitimate ambition." I mean even Gordon Gekko told us that greed was good in *Wall Street*. But did even Gekko believe that? No one is saying you can't have a level of self-interest but surely it must combine, or at least chime, with the interests of others. Paul couldn't have put it more clearly. Let each of us not look to our own interests but to the interests of others, he said (Phil 2:4). Nothing there about it being okay to have an S Class Mercedes if you can do with an E Class—and give the difference to that irritating bloke on the other side of the road. So whether you are stuffing your face with that extra bar (guilty) or are selfish and greedy at work, play, and toward others (oops . . . guilty again), let us try and remember the wise if somewhat uncomfortable words of German psychologist Erich Fromm: "Greed is a bottomless pit which exhausts the person in an endless effort to satisfy the need without ever reaching satisfaction."[2] If that isn't telling, I don't know what is.

Incidentally, if you think this has all got a bit heavy, the deadly sin coming up? Lust. Please don't say you weren't warned.

---

2. Erich Fromm, "More Quotes by Erich Fromm," ForbesQuotes, https://www.forbes.com/quotes/author/erich-fromm.

Lust?

It's a Tricky One . . .

I WARNED READERS IN PREVIOUS pages that this deadly sin could be the most problematic of all. I mean, what exactly could I say about lust without getting myself into trouble? Well buckle up, ladies and gentlemen, and prepare for trouble with a capital T, and maybe even lust with a rather large L. Let's start off gently, shall we, with a simple definition. According to the *Cambridge Dictionary*, lust is "a very strong sexual desire."[1] There, I've said it. Well at least the dictionary said it and there is no easy way around that four letter world that appears to make the world go round, or not, depending on your point of view. And when it comes to lust, there are many points of view. Apparently for most under-thirties in the mid-2020s all is fine on that front and, sure, whatever you're having yourself goes. God made us this way and there is not a lot we can do about it. To a greater or lesser extent, and at various points in our lives, we are all lustful creatures and you can hardly blame us for that. Young people (and some older ones) have seemingly little else on their minds. It's a wonder we can get to work, go shopping, or clean the kitchen on a Saturday. Not so much *50 Shades of Grey*, more 1,000 shades of scarlet. We are on the Lust Train, destination, Sodom and Begorrah (that one is for Irish readers only).

Okay, let's row back a bit. There are essentially two attitudes out there to sexual activity. The first we are told is the most popular. Sex is a consumerist activity and should be chosen as one would a bottle of wine or the latest mobile phone. Fine while it lasts but then it's time to move on and see if there is a finer wine or an upgraded phone to purchase. The other attitude, allegedly less prevalent, is that lust and sex are an activity of connection and

---

1. *Cambridge Advanced Learner's Dictionary and Thesaurus*, "Lust," Cambridge Dictionary, https://dictionary.cambridge.org/dictionary/english/lust.

possibly, dare we even say it, love. In the criminal world, men who sexually offend may display either. Some will brazenly label their offense an act of mere consumption but others will suggest that it was an act of love, albeit neither the victim nor society sees it that way. Both remain offenders notwithstanding their presentational spin. You see when it comes to searching for a uniform attitude to lust, humanity is in something of a tailspin of its own making.

What does the Bible have to say about lust? Well quite a lot as it happens, though many think the biblical view on lust and related activities are really for the birds (and bees?) and God would not have given us the power of lust if he did not intend for us to be... well... lustful. It's a neat argument but not the full story by any manner of means. Not committing adultery (Exod 20:14)? Well, that's less contentious. However, in something of a Scriptural backflip (and slightly more controversially), if you cannot exercise self-control, Corinthians tells us, then you should get married, for it is better to do so than to burn with passion (1 Cor 7:9). Simply being highly sexually charged does seem like a less than noble reason to get married.

And perhaps most controversial of all comes Matthew when he says that any man who looks at a woman with lustful intent has already committed adultery with her in his heart (Matt 5:28). One assumes the same applies to women, incidentally. In fairness to Matthew, that is a theological pin-drop moment. What exactly can that statement possibly mean and how can we apply it to our natural human instincts? The Bible has something of a history of being open to interpretation. Some Christian denominations, too, have a habit of welcoming dissenting voices into their theological gymnastics, so that much of the time we take from passages what we may provided we are not obviously making it up as we go along. This passage however can surely only have one interpretation. Forget about being lustful *with* anyone. This is telling us we cannot even *think* lustfully, for that is the exact same thing as if we had acted out. This is important news. I mean, not even the criminal law goes that far, so why Matthew and others? Like a lot of biblical messages, the reason is staring us right in the face. Matthew's passage is usually roundly dismissed and ignored by the younger generation, and even the older generation, who regard it as a piece of Scripture they can park as it's just a little off message. The truth? Matthew could not be more *on* message if he tried.

A good starting point are criminals. They often are. Many sex offenders (despite their protests) view sexual activity, and its predecessor, lust, as

Part 2: The Seven Deadly Sins

a simple act of consuming a product. Zero connectivity, no emotionality, and a total absence of any warmth or love. Of course it's not just criminal offenders who take that view of the sexual arena as their playground. Much of humanity still seems to regard it all as harmless fun with no repercussions for either party, or indeed wider society. To believe otherwise (so the script goes) is old-fashioned, impractical, and frankly goes against a person's "right" to do what they want with their own thoughts and body.

Yet it is Matthew who goes to the heart of what it means to be human and have respect for other humans. Scripture preaches love, nothing more, nothing less. Random and plentiful lustful thoughts and actions are the opposite of love, for such thoughts regard each person toward whom these feelings are directed, as mere objects to satisfy the lustful person's desire. They have no intrinsic value, yet they are being used by those of us who are told by our faith to "love" and only love. Though we may not like it, the truth is that random lustful thoughts are loathsome thoughts. The good news however is there is no part of the Bible that bans sexual activity and its surrounding emotions, once it's within its faith-led context. If you don't believe me, try Song of Songs with its candid, if not at times almost explicit sexual poetry. Lust and sexual activity by definition have their place in God's plan, but here's the shocker. It should be practiced within one loving relationship where the other person is not a commodity but a companion, not simply an object of desire, but someone who is loved.

Matthew was ahead of the posse when it came to lust. It is *because* we have respect for each other that we should not see other humans as bit players in our lustful storyboard. Lust and sex are not distinct from emotion and love, and despite our protests and attempts to do so (are you listening men) they never were and never will be, for that is how we were made by the one who knows.

Now if you will excuse me, it's time for me to think about envy next. And you thought lust was awkward.

Envy
The Slipperiest of Serpents

GROWING UP, I WAS a peculiar little chap. No surprise there I hear you say but bear with me. I always had this strange sense of my own worth which you might think was a solid base for an odd child with an inexplicable obsession with newsreaders and female shot-putters. How wrong you would be. My self-regard reached such heights in my childhood that in primary school I would suggest to the teacher that I begin reading Ladybird Book 9a, when the class was only on 2b. A nice offer but based on no evidence whatsoever that I could read 2b properly, let alone 9a. The teacher would indulge me, and then I would be told to sit down as I had the book the wrong way around. You would think that such public humiliation might, as we say in Ireland, have softened my cough somewhat, but not a bit of it. By the time I was entering secondary school I had, in the manner of Donald Trump, made myself great, notwithstanding the evidence that, yet again, everything was pointing to the contrary. From singing to football and back to all school subjects, I was the best and the rest of the herd were simply playing catch-up. I blame my late parents. You keep telling your child they really are the best and they will eventually believe you until such time as the rest of the world starts to offer a different opinion. Mind you, if they've done a good enough job of convincing you, you'll be impervious to that, too. Cheers, Mum and Dad.

So why I am telling you all of this in relation to the deadly sin of envy? Well one of the plus sides of being told you are the best and then genuinely believing it is that you are never truly envious of anyone or anything. In the game of snakes and ladders that is life, the fact that loads of people around you may be throwing a six while you keep rolling a one or two and sliding down yet another ladder is neither here nor there. If you are (genuinely)

Part 2: The Seven Deadly Sins

confident enough, you will wish them all well and continue basking in your own self-reflected glory, regardless of life's outcomes. Don't get me wrong, it's not that those in that situation don't have another different set of problems, and, yes, before you ask, my psychiatrist says I am doing very well.

The difficulty with envy however is that it comes from a place of catastrophic low self-esteem. These were the kids who, unlike me, were told they most certainly were not the best, or at least they felt they were not. Unlike jealously, which is more in your face, envy lurks in the shadows, in the darker nooks and crannies of our mind where someone else's perceived elevation in life can only mean one thing. The envious person's deflation. Of course often we will dress our envy up as something else. We will give it a catwalk strut that makes our actions more acceptable to ourselves and others. And its subtle. You put someone down? Well they deserved it; they were wrong on that matter. You provoke a situation and then you stand back and enjoy the fireworks you have lit? You use sarcasm toward another, but dress it up as humor, but the victim doesn't laugh? Well they just couldn't take the "joke." Yet all the time it seems to be the envious person who can't understand the joke.

Marrying your own success or failure to that of others is never going to end well, of course. Envy will always seek to either destroy or ruin in some way what another person has. We may deeply want their car, holidays, jobs, possessions, or their cosy and apparently flawless family life. We dreamed of the 2.5 kids and the picket fence in the countryside but all we got was a damp, urban bedsit and a feral cat staring at us as we eat our reheated meal from Aldi (other reheats are available). It wasn't exactly how we predicted it all turning out, and in many ways no one can blame such persons for their "compare and despair" moments. It's a poor "victory" though. Hoping for, or even engineering the downfall of another, eats you up inside like nothing else can. You lose, they lose, yet all this almost certainly comes from a childhood in which early important needs were not met. And you guessed it, our best guide of all, Scripture, has a few things to say on the matter. The core passages are the bits we are meant to know inside out, and practice, by the way.

You remember that stuff about not coveting your neighbor's ox (Range Rover), their house (in Beverly Hills), their wife (WAG, or otherwise), or, for the avoidance of any doubt, *anything* that is your neighbor's? Thank you, Exodus, for your clarity but for many of us we appear to have put that to one side for now. For here is a bit of envy we prepared earlier and, sure, it's nothing more than those "successful" people deserve. Let's not put too fine a point on it. Those of us who envy (among other things) will not see God's kingdom according to Gal 5:19–21, for where envy is, every evil thing exists (Jas 3:16). And, for the avoidance of any doubt, Proverbs reminds us that envy is rottenness to our bones (14:30). So the one deadly sin that many of us have relegated to the lower league of offenses, appears in fact to be one of critical scriptural import.

As ever though, while we might have let God down, he has not abandoned us in our envious slitherings, and the answer as always is love, for love does not envy (1 Cor 13:4) as it is the bond of perfection (Col 3:14). Perhaps, firstly, we ought to start loving ourselves as the psychologists and counselors might say, before we can begin to cease our envious ways and start to love those most who may deserve it least. Or you could, of course, adopt the Deane-O'Keeffe school of childhood thought and simply convince yourself you are the best. Trust me, you'll never suffer from envious thoughts, at least. Other stuff? Guaranteed.

Now if you will excuse me I need to go to my local McDonald's for a sit-down large Big Mac meal with extra fries to consider our next deadly sin. Gluttony. Now stop. What have I told you about envy?

Gluttony
Have We Bitten Off More Than We Can Chew?

MY LATE MOTHER HAD a number of go to dislikes. She particularly didn't care much for smaller women, or, indeed, larger. The irony of this was not lost on the rest of the family as mother was five feet on a good day, and she would never turn down a large roast herself, followed by a large bowl of Angel Delight. And that was just for breakfast. While it's something of a tired old trope to note that those who dislike their own appearance tend to point to those very features in others, it made me conscious of speed-eating and general gluttony over the years. You would be forgiven for thinking, therefore, that this would subsequently ensure I would enjoy my food with the pace and serenity of a Trappist monk. Not a bit of it. Gluttony? I may have invented it and, although to this day I resemble more of a boa constrictor at mealtimes than a prayerful hermit, I prefer to firmly position myself in the George Bernard Shaw camp, when he said, "There is no love sincerer than the love of food."[1] At least that's my story, and I'm sticking to it.

Although gluttony has always been something more than excessive eating, it is still most certainly that. Aquinas saw gluttony as an "inordinate desire"[2] and the Bible, too, says that for the enemies of the gospel, "their God is their stomach" (Phil 3:19). "Those who keep the law are wise children, but companions of gluttons shame their parents" (Prov 28:7). I also

---

1. George Bernard Shaw, *Man and Superman: A Comedy and a Philosophy* (New York: Heritage, 1962), 18.

2. Thomas Aquinas, "Question 148—Gluttony: Article 1—Whether Gluttony Is a Sin," in *Summa Theologiae*, 2nd rev. ed., trans. Fathers of the English Dominican Province (London: Burns, Oates and Washbourne, 1920), New Advent, 2017, https://www.newadvent.org/summa/3148.htm#article1.

Gluttony

came across Paul's words on the matter recently and, as a Licensed Minister, I think it may be time for some reflection. He was afraid of being disbarred from ministry if he did not care for his body by physically disciplining it from gluttonous excess (1 Cor 9:27). Yikes.

Young people today know all about the challenges of being accused of gluttony. On the one hand, there remain a cohort out there who think all they have to be is "skinny" and life's rewards will be plentiful. On the other, are a newer group who think that gluttonous excess with all its attendant physical problems is a personal choice and is equally rewarding. In truth, there seems to be no certain pathway for the young (and not so young) when it comes to food and their appearance. Rest easy young people of the world. The debate was ever so. While Jesus Christ himself was erroneously accused of being a glutton (Luke 7:34) elsewhere John the Baptist was regarded as having been possessed by the devil because he did *not* gorge himself (Luke 7:33). Even in biblical times you couldn't win when it came to your diet. Some things never change. While gluttony may not be directly mentioned in the Bible as a sin, we probably shouldn't be in any doubt that it is. Especially when it gets thrown into the "lust of the flesh" group of problems (1 Cor 6:19–20).

Of course it's not the food per se that's the scriptural problem. God wants us to enjoy the healthy and plentiful variety of food that the earth supplies us with, and indeed the Bible is replete with stories of feasts, many of which Jesus himself attended. The issue is one of moderation in all things and care for our bodies as both reveal a respect for ourselves and for our God. The problem is in the excessive worship of food which, like all addictions, will distract and subvert our love for him. Yet, modern audiences please additionally note, the Bible dislikes those who judge others' relationships with food and like to pass comment on it (Rom 14), for their appearance may have nothing to do with gluttony, albeit that is what we believe. Frankly, it's all none of our business.

Perhaps a better prism for contemporary congregations when it comes to gluttony is to look at overeating as we might overindulgence in anything in our lives, and how such behaviors fracture our relationship with ourselves, others, and, of course, God. No one has any issue saying, for example, that scourges like drugs, alcohol, pornography, and the world's infatuation with social media and mobile phones are all forms of obsession, addiction, and even idolatry. When it comes to that extra-large packet of fries, however, well, perhaps understandably, we are more flexible. Yet the principle surely remains the same. And it is our worldly obsessions of all sorts, including our gluttonous lifestyles and habits, that are tripping us Christians up. Without wishing to state the obvious, when all the "Mercs and perks" are set aside, when we finally slump in our chairs and our lives are now beside us, where will we say we got our joys as we come before the Christ we purport to know and love? Will it be the night (sorry, nights) we gorged ourselves in that restaurant after those golf functions? Or maybe the amount of times we cooked and ate up a storm when hosting and attending those dinners parties and soirees, only to then end up throwing most of the food in the bin? Hardly.

Doubtless, this world offers us many, many temporary and empty pursuits, including food. And trust me when I say that there are few people who probably know this better than this writer. God is hiding in full view for us every day and yet we cannot see him properly. He is waiting for us to satisfy our souls, not our bellies, yet still if we had a choice between spending a couple of hours in a local prayer group or a night of feasting in a three-star Michelin restaurant, who might win? Well, I'm going to suggest that most of the time, God might just miss out on the pleasure of our company for that evening. Admittedly there may be *worse* sins. Try homicide or serious violence, for starters, but this is hardly the point. By diverting out attention, our worship, our joy, and our pleasures away from God and toward the corpulent delights of food excess or culinary bingeing, we do a huge disservice to both ourselves and our faith. Our belief cannot, in the words of Phil Collins, be a part-time love, and, trust me, giant burgers can get in the way.

Remember, this *is* it, ladies and gentlemen, for this time is our time, our one moment to shine and reflect God's love for us and his creation with all others we meet, and in all things we do. While they undoubtedly have their charms, obsessive guzzling of family boxes in Kentucky Fried Chicken or supersize-me Big Macs in McDonald's (other junk foods are available) are not considered normative pathways to God.

Maybe mother was right after all. So please, all now put your hands in the air and back slowly away from that McFlurry. Remember, she's watching you.

Sloth?

Cut Your Sloth to Suit Your Measure

WHEN I WAS A boy (and stop laughing over in the corner, Madam, I was once), I had an uncanny ability to sleep anywhere, anytime. Beds, broomsticks, bus shelters, and bogs, you name it, I could sleep on or near it. As a student it got worse. Come 2:00 p.m. I might still not be up, and the family would be about to call an ambulance to check for any vital signs, and then I would appear to many looking, for all the world, as if I had spent a week digging roads. I had, in fact, done absolutely nothing, zero, but I was a student, and until you are one you have no idea how exhausting it can be going (or in my case, not going) to six hours of lectures a week. I could be woken on those days, but at a push. When I was allegedly a student, on July 19, 1984, an earthquake hit Wales and the east coast of Ireland at 7:57 a.m. that was of sufficient strength, and brace yourselves for this, it actually managed to wake up me. I never even knew at that point in my life that people actually went to a thing called work at that time of day when I looked out the window. Ridiculous. Once the earthquake passed I went back to bed, as you do. No one did lazy like John. Believe me.

Which, of course, all got me to thinking about that deadly sin of sloth. A hugely ignored sin, but obviously highly regarded by me back in the day. Dictionary definitions can be helpful at this point. The *Cambridge Dictionary* definition advises that it is "an animal that moves very slowly and spends much of its time hanging by its feet from trees."[1] Tick box. Alternatively, it is someone who is unwilling to work or make any effort. In the 1980s, therefore, I would have managed to satisfy both fairly effortlessly. So what really is the big deal about *working* anyway? Why bother if you

---

1. *Cambridge Advanced Learner's Dictionary and Thesaurus*, "Sloth," Cambridge Dictionary, https://dictionary.cambridge.org/dictionary/english/sloth.

can get away without doing any and survive? Leaving aside those who are sadly unable to work for very good reason, what about the rest? You know, the professional limp fishes who live on either the state, family, friends, or sometimes, if they are experts, on all three. Perhaps it's all just bitterness on the rest of our parts—and aren't we the fools anyway for doing the work in the first place? Perhaps, but it's a bit more complex.

From a non-religious perspective there are many good reasons to work and avoid slothfulness, not least of which are financial ones. There are also, of course, the mental health benefits for what we call "personal significance" and "cognitive closure," which in plain English mean we have our, "because we are worth it" moments, and we feel we have completed and done a task or job well. We are fairly simple creatures, really. Then it can go a bit deeper. Working well and for the good of others as well as ourselves sets an excellent example for our children. Attempting to access why adults commit crimes, we will always go back to the childhood in my academic discipline. Were the parents criminal? Then the children are more likely to be criminal. It's not nuclear physics and its goes for every behavior we exhibit and which they soak up. Live off the state when you don't have to? Guess what? They probably will too. Go out to work every day because you respect yourself and your family? You've got it. All things being equal, the kids will probably end up doing the same. The reality is, you do as you see.

Which kind of takes us to the next level when looking at sloth. What does Christ think of our ability to "sloth it out" when everyone else around us appears to be getting on with things? I'm afraid it's bad news for young versions of me out there (on so many levels). He doesn't like it for us. I'll tell you where Christ really doesn't like it. The Book of Proverbs. Granted if you're already slothful, you probably haven't got the energy to read any book of the Bible, let alone it, but I still direct you to Proverbs in your more active moments.

No punches pulled here. The soul of the laggard craves and gets nothing (Prov 13:4), his way is like a hedge of thorns (15:19), and because he does not plough in the autumn, he will seek at harvest but have nothing (20:4). It gets worse. The slothful person is like vinegar to the teeth and smoke to the eyes (10:26) and, with more than an uncanny pointer to my youth, as the door turns on its hinges, so does a sluggard on his bed (26:14). None of this is sounding promising from a biblical perspective, and even in the occasionally more upbeat 1 Timothy, we are advised that if we don't provide for members of our house, then we have denied the faith and are

Sloth?

worse than an unbeliever (1 Tim 5:8). Avoiding slothfulness in our modern lives is about far more than bringing home the bread, paying the bills, and having our cars and holidays, though it is all that as well. It goes far deeper, however. It is a witness to Christ's love and respect when we take up any job whatsoever we do each day and do it well, in his name.

Come to think of it, maybe we should go back to biblical basics on all of this. And where better to begin than in Genesis? The first book tells us very clearly that God took the man and put him in the garden of Eden to work it and keep it (Gen 2:15). Work, howsoever it looks, is good for us, good for our family and friends and those we know and influence, good for ourselves, and, most of all, good for our relationship with God. That each of us may eat, drink, and find satisfaction in all our toil? That is the gift from God (Eccl 3:13).

Don't get me wrong. Slothfulness may sometimes have its place, especially in campuses around the globe as young people settle into their student lives. Probably best to complement it with some work as well though, young students out there. And if you want clarity on this, by the way, you may like to ask your parents. Now if you will excuse me, all this talk of work has somewhat exhausted me. Sure, what possible harm is forty winks for a tired preacher?

Postscript: Cardinal Virtues
Don't Perspire the Small Sins

I KNOW. YOU'RE EXHAUSTED. ALL you heard from me above are all the bad things. From lust, wrath, and greed, right back around to pride, envy, gluttony, and sloth, we have been on the deadly sins roller coaster, destination, fiery abyss. Reasonably, you are now dusting yourself down and asking John to lighten up. A fair point, so let me now introduce, in the blue corner, the four cardinal virtues of prudence, justice, fortitude, and temperance. I mean, what could possibly go wrong? These are virtues, and all we have to do is to try to adhere to them, right? "Awks," as the young people might say.

Unlike the seven deadly sins, we have some nice backup on the four cardinal virtues, namely in Song 8:7: "And if anyone loves righteousness, her labours are virtues; for she teaches self-control and prudence, justice and courage; nothing in life is more profitable for mortals than these." Quite. One small issue before we ask if we are any good at them, however: Do we even agree on what they mean? Is one man's prudence another man's meanness? Is another's justice someone else's ethnic cleansing? Does fortitude mean resilience to one person, and stubbornness to another? Could it even be that temperance is moderation to her, while he thinks it's just giving up alcohol for Lent?

Mind you, prudence is one word we don't hear too much of anymore in any event. "That Pamela is fiercely prudent" is not typical language one hears in the rolling hills of Fermanagh and South Tyrone, much less the mean streets of Seattle or Shanghai. Of course, it normally means we are marked with wisdom of some sort and that can't be a bad thing, but, being humans, we have managed to turn its meaning around. Nowadays if someone is ever referred to as prudent, it's generally a polite way of saying

Postscript: Cardinal Virtues

they're mean. How did that happen? The following is instructive. My wife came back from a trip some time ago to England where she had spent a weekend with some ladies she knew and their friends. She described a moment where one of their number was trying to work out how much dessert another lady had eaten from another's unfinished one, so as to work out the precise amount she now owed on the bill. That's prudence, Jim, but not as we know it. You see, prudence is easy enough to understand if we stopped reinventing what it means. The Bible gives us a helping hand as ever, for "the simple believe everything, but the clever consider their steps" (Prov 14:15). Let's not confuse it with being a tad boring or frugal. We have, after all, plenty of other words for that.

Justice sounds much easier, right? Again, what could possibly go wrong? After all, surely none of us disagree over its meaning which we might boil down to a simple fairness in the treatment of people. Easy, eh? The problem is if we were to ask Palestinians or Israelis today their definition of justice, we would find two very different interpretations. Russia and Ukraine, the same, and on it goes. Gospel translators tend to veer toward righteousness, another word we all love and believe we understand, even if we really don't. Perhaps you can't blame us. Something which is "morally right or just" is, after all, about as movable a set of goalposts as you could assemble. Try geopolitics in the Middle East, Sudan, or Ukraine, to name but three. See what I mean?

Thankfully we then have fortitude. Again, not a descriptor you hear too much today. But why not? It's dead easy, after all. It's courage in pain or adversity, and in Scripture we know that a woman, for example, with fortitude "girds herself with strength, and makes her arms strong" (Prov 31:17). Yet no one seems to pay much attention to it nowadays and, in fact, vulnerability may be the new fortitude. A sound development in one very important sense, but it does seem a shame that the potential for our inner strength may have been cast out in the process.

Then there is temperance. Being temperate seems a no-brainer when it comes to universal understanding but, as already mentioned, even it can get sidelined into simply showing moderation or abstinence when it comes to drink, which is kind of to miss the broader, more interesting point. During Christmas 2006, as I was walking up to greet Pogues front man Shane McGowan in the Four Seasons hotel in Dublin, he uttered the immortal words to his minder, "Please get that [expletive] drunk away from me." Needless to say, after such a public dressing down from one of the world's finest drinkers, I have been fully abstinent ever since.

Part 2: The Seven Deadly Sins

So in times of temptation (i.e., always), the four cardinal virtues may actually be the hardest roll call we may ever have to answer. Prudence? Likely to be thrown out the window as we live in various moments of excess. Justice? See how much we truly reflect on injustice around the world as we tuck into our Easter dinner, Christmas turkey, or Thanksgiving goose? Fortitude? Life has a habit of breaking our abilities to show strength in the face of some inevitable adversity. Temperance? Whatever way we define it, I think we all know that isn't going to happen every day.

So there you were thinking that those nice cardinal virtues would come along and wrap us in warm, cozy cloaks as we banished those seven deadly sins to the sinning rubbish bin. Perhaps in one way the sins are easier for us. It's the virtues (cardinal or otherwise) that are the really difficult bit, but the answer may be even closer than we think. Yes, Madam, you've got it. Love. That one-word Leviathan can, and maybe should, be the answer to both the cardinal sins and virtues. Indeed, perhaps *sins* and *virtues* are faulty prisms in which to navigate our Christian lives in any event. Maybe we should all just concentrate on that love and compassion thing for this month and every month and see where it gets us.

Mind you. Not that Christmas is much fun for me anymore since 2006. Punk-rock legend, Shane McGowan made sure of that . . .

Part 3
Take 5: Sermonettes from the Shade

Are You a Thermometer or Thermostat Person?
Testing the Temperature in Spring

February is a bit of a tragic month. Let me explain. This is the second month of the year in the Julian and Georgian calendars. So far, so good. However, on the one hand the meteorological calendar tells us that Spring begins in March, while St Brigid's Day on the 1st February is considered the beginning of Spring in the Celtic calendar. Now you might be saying to me John, what of it? Sure, we have more to be worrying about.

Well, I'll tell you madam. The first problem is that us reformed types are very literal people and we still have in our heads that Spring begins in February, despite all the evidence to the contrary such as Polar Bears dropping dead of the cold in New York, Dublin & London (other areas are available). God help us but there's your Churchwarden sauntering down the road in his Speedos in the first week in February, only to make a quick retreat to retrieve his full length winter mink coat. I know, quite an image but you know what those Churchwardens are like.

Secondly and more importantly, the cold month of February always gets me thinking about temperature and how we approach it more generally in our lives. A banker once said to me that you are either a 'thermometer' person or a 'thermostat' person in this world. The 'thermometer' people take the temperature of the other people of the room they are in, and react accordingly. The 'thermostat' people on the other hand set the temperature of the room and everyone else settles into that number. In others words one is led, the other leads.

It really sounds like some awful away day corporate speak doesn't it? Simple division of the human condition into two types, and yet it is not

Part 3: Take 5: Sermonettes from the Shade

without some credibility. There are some of us after all who are more reactive than others and follow the group and there are others who prefer to set the pace and lead. Which group you may or may not fall into (or perhaps even both) may have some bearing on how you or others navigate your life but ultimately its meaningless in the eyes of God.

Were we kind? Were we compassionate? Did we visit your fellow humans when they were in prison, or were sick? Did we love? Most of all, were we authentic in all the above? For as Christ Himself says, as you did it to one of the least of my brethren, you did it to me. So it might be worth us all talking the temperature test every February—and many during a few other months as well. How are we when it comes to our faith? Hot or cold? Take out the thermometer and check. I'm guessing for most of us, we could probably then do with turning up that thermostat.

Now if you will excuse me, I see our Churchwarden is texting me. Apparently there is a two for one offer on fake fur in our local clothing store. I know. Impossible to refuse.

Money Can't Buy You Love

ENVY IS A WONDERFUL gift, in which case it must be my birthday every day. There I was, delighted with myself, getting on the ferry at Holyhead in Wales in my car after seven long weeks hanging out of the dreamy spires of Oxford. As I rolled on, I thought my vehicle looked quite the part, too. A black Lexus SUV with cream leather seats and a dash of interior ivory trim, no less. Okay, fair enough, it's over a decade old, but I was surely a person to be reckoned with and nobody, but nobody, could spoil my mood. That was, of course, until I found myself on the lower deck wedged between a Bentley Azure (with an absolute abundance of leather trim) and a new Range Rover Vogue. My green-eyed monster could deal with the Bentley. It was an English registration after all. And, sure, he would have one, wouldn't he? No, what really got my goat up was the brand new Range Rover behind me which not only had an Irish registration but also the chap that then jumped out of it. Honestly, I think I have socks older than him. Which doesn't say a lot for my sock collection, I admit, but you get the point. As I stumbled my way up to the hoi polloi lounge, I couldn't help but think what my late mother once said to me about money. "Money gives you dignity, John," she would say. She might have had a point. Those two lads jumping down off their "Chelsea tractors" certainly looked as if they had buckets of that dignity thing all right.

But we get the general thrust of her words. Money may not be able to buy you love, but it can sort the monthly bills and mortgage and keep your children in clothes and warmth. That's dignity. It's also true to say that the people who say money doesn't matter generally have enough themselves, so it doesn't. To them. However, there is of course another side to it too. There does come a point in our obsession with the earning and harvesting of filthy lucre where we go well past that point of dignity and get mired in the undignified. Of course, Christ himself was drawn to the poor, not the rich, except in so far as he could warn the fat cats against placing an overemphasis on worldly possessions as against their faith. So once we hit that sweet spot of financial dignity, then we, too, surely need to calm down and ask ourselves, Why *do* we still want more?

If it's to give to charity and/or put notes at regular intervals into someone's mendicant hand on the street (without then directing how *you* think it should be spent) then well done, you, for Christ will most certainly approve. If it's to get a Bentley or Range Rover, however, then please don't. Remember, I'm still recovering from the last two I saw.

Credible or Incredible?

Now not a lot of people know this, but May is the anniversary of the Loch Ness Monster's first sighting in 1933. A couple of months later that year a married couple also claimed to have seen the creature with the husband suggesting that it was "the nearest [thing] to a dragon or prehistoric animal that I have ever seen in my life."[1] Which does somewhat beg the question, precisely how *many* prehistoric creatures had he seen in his life? His description of the animal was even more curious as one which had "a long neck, which moved up and down in the manner of a scenic railway." I know what you're thinking. Trainspotters, eh? So it's all very easy to be skeptical of George Spicer and his missus, and indeed all who were to follow on the trail of the Loch Ness Monster. A giant creature in a Scottish lake? Well I've never heard the like. Anyway, it's the ones standing on the shoreline you should probably keep a closer eye on. Yet it's not just alleged Loch monsters that can send some of us into a skeptical frenzy. Try religion, and especially religiously fervent folk.

Which segues me neatly to our May anniversary. Alongside Nessie, every year on May 13, we celebrate the feast day of St. Julian of Norwich. And before you ask, no, this wasn't a man. Juliana, to be precise, and one of the best known anchoresses (a type of stay-at-home hermit) of her day, and possibly since. Not the life for me, I hear you cry. And while we are probably all agreed that this was niche even for its day, withdrawing into prayer for life because of a love of Christ isn't exactly off the Christian message.

---

1. Neil J. Gostling, "Why the Search for the Loch Ness Monster (and Other Beasts) Continues 90 Years After That First Blurry Photograph," Conversation, Nov. 10, 2023, https://theconversation.com/why-the-search-for-the-loch-ness-monster-and-other-beasts-continues-90-years-after-that-first-blurry-photograph-217475.

Part 3: Take 5: Sermonettes from the Shade

Where Juliana did, however, receive public incredulity at the time and since was due to the revelations she claimed she had of Christ, experiences she had during a near-fatal illness, and which she subsequently turned into her magnum opus, *Revelations of Divine Love*. Juliana had three big problems if she wanted to be believed. Firstly, she was a woman (fatal at the time), secondly, she was an allegedly uneducated one (doubly fatal), and thirdly, she was gravely ill (so must have been having hallucinations). All in all, for many, therefore, right up there with the Loch Ness Monster on the believability index.

The reality is we will never know for certain if Juliana had real spiritual encounters with Christ or, indeed, honest if imagined versions—or perhaps none at all. This much we do know, however. The deeply theological writings of St. Julian of Norwich meant that she surely resisted being known by anybody *other* than God. We all journey to God. How so? By love, of course, she says, for love was his meaning, and that alone is why "all shall be well."

Which is probably more than can be said for poor Nessie's credibility.

When We Didn't Have Your Hands, We Had Your Backs

If I were to ask you what was the significance of June 16, some readers might answer its Bloomsday, the day that commemorates Leopold Bloom's walk and encounters across Dublin in 1904. Here, the ordinary became the extraordinary and no one noticed the seam. As the young folk might say, "Whatever." Surely of far greater import however in any year is that June is the month for Father's Day. That's right, ladies and gentlemen, it's time to start buying those presents right now for me to celebrate how great I am. And if you don't believe me, ask one of my five children. On second thoughts, sure, just take my word for it. No need to start confusing matters now, is there?

But we poor dads remain second best when it comes to our big day. Mother's Day was established back in the early 1900s but Father's Day did not become a recognized holiday in the US until as recently as 1972. Mother's Day gets celebrated first in May and the poor old dads have to wait until June. Roses of all colors are the flower of Mother's Day, while Father's Day traditionally get associated with the poor man's roses: sunflowers. To make matters worse, roses used to be the flower of Father's Day, that is until the mothers moved in. Americans spend some $22 billion annually on Father's Day,[1] which sounds great until you realize the mothers have won again,

---

1. Sara Chernikoff and Jennifer Borresen, "How Much Do You Spend on Father's Day Gifts? Americans Favor Mom over Dad, Survey Says," *USA Today*, June 15, 2024, https://eu.usatoday.com/story/news/nation/2024/06/15/how-much-do-americans-spend-on-fathers-day/74065402007.

as they get upward of $34 billion spent on their big day.[2] And to top it all, research has suggested that about 58 percent of Father's Day "presents" are a greeting card.[3] Gosh, thanks kids, what we always wanted. I mean, if you were bitter in any way (myself included) you might begin to believe that your role may not be considered as important as that of mother.

I jest, of course, and, critically, fathers underestimate the importance of their behaviors and actions to their children's upbringing at their peril. Research tells us that supportive fathers have children with higher levels of emotional resilience, self-esteem, and well-being. Good attempts at being a father will normally mean better mental health, higher educational attainment, greater economic stability, and healthier romantic relationships in adulthood for all our kids. Note the word *good*, not *excellent*. None of us are perfect fathers (or mothers, for that matter), but perhaps many of us might be nearer what the pop psychologists call "Goldilocks" or "just right" parents. We get things wrong, we get things right, but, in the end, things generally turn out okay. And *okay* is really great, and most of us fathers are *okay*. Perhaps it was us, and not James Joyce, who all along were the ones who really made the ordinary, extraordinary.

So a message for my children. No need for any presents in any June for me. You were, are, and always will be the greatest ones I could ever have. Now, of course, if you still did want to throw some cash into the card . . .

---

2. Kasia Davies, "Mother's Day Expenditure in the U.S. 2007–2024," Statista, Jan. 14, 2025, www.statista.com/statistics/289496/us-mother-s-day-expenditure.

3. Chernikoff and Borresen, "How Much Do You Spend?"

And They Call It Puppy Love . . .

O KAY. HANDS UP ALL of you who have children/grandchildren in summer camps last year or coming up. Or were there yourself back in the day. Noted. That's all of you, so, good, I can begin. It was Carna, Connemara, County Galway, Ireland, and the year was 1977, and her name was Mary. Unfortunately I was thirteen at the time and Mary didn't know what had hit her until she met me. I immediately decided I wanted to marry her, which was admittedly an unusual life choice for a thirteen-year-old, but I was always focused, even from an early age. I wooed her over those three weeks in the way only a young gentleman in platform shoes, corduroy trousers, a cheesecloth shirt, and with more than a bang of nasty after-shave about him can. Think Leslie McKeown (tartan-clad lead singer of the Bay City Rollers) crossed with Karen Carpenter and you've got me. I really was quite the sight.

The three weeks ended before they began and I said my farewells to her at the train station in Galway. Not before, however, I would give her my parting gift. My claddagh ring. As the train pulled away from the station, I yanked the ring from my hand to give to her only for Mary to brush it away in utter horror while we both watched as it fell between the tracks. Not so much a Dr. Zhivago as a Dr. Who moment. I must have looked some spectacle as I forlornly walked back from the platform to await my own Dublin-bound train. This was rejection, but on a biblical scale.

Falling in love as a teenager is a disaster of Herculean dimensions (note to file: it can have its moments later in life too). To make matters worse, everyone smiles when you do and tells you it will be fine and "there are plenty more fish in the sea." Well, if there were, they weren't swimming toward me. Christ knew better than most about the potential love that children and younger people have within their hearts and, indeed, the love that comes from their parents. After all, God so loved the world that he gave his own Son to be with and die for us, and Matthew tells us that if we wish to enter God's kingdom, then we too need to become like little children (18:3).

So if you want to know what "falling in love" means to a teenager you should have no problem. Just remember when you were one and what it felt like when you were either on top of the world or in the pits of teenage, lovelorn despair. Now expect a selection of those children or grandchildren back from various camps with either one of those looks on their faces.

As for Mary? A message. All I can say to you now, Mary, is that you had a very lucky escape. Then again, you surely know that now.

www.ingramcontent.com/pod-product-compliance
Lightning Source LLC
Chambersburg PA
CBHW071428160426
43195CB00013B/1842